ACONCAGUA: SOUTH FACE

Left to right:

    (*Seated*) LUCIEN BERARDINI, PIERRE LESUEUR, EDMOND DENIS.
    (*Standing*) GUY POULET, ROBERT PARAGOT, SUZANNE & RÉNÉ
             FERLET, ADRIEN DAGORY

ACONCAGUA:
SOUTH FACE

by

RÉNÉ FERLET and GUY POULET

Translated from the French by
E. NOEL BOWMAN
F.R.G.S., Member of the Alpine Club

with Illustrations

LONDON:
CONSTABLE & COMPANY LIMITED
ORANGE STREET W.C.2

LONDON
PUBLISHED BY
Constable and Company Ltd
10-12 ORANGE STREET W.C.2

INDIA
Orient Longmans Ltd
BOMBAY CALCUTTA MADRAS

CANADA
Longmans, Green and Company
TORONTO

SOUTH *and* EAST AFRICA
Longmans, Green and Company Ltd
CAPETOWN   NAIROBI

AUSTRALIA
Walter Standish and Sons
SYDNEY

First published 1956

Printed in Great Britain by Richard Clay and Company, Ltd.,
Bungay, Suffolk.

We dedicate this narrative

to

GENERAL JUAN DOMINGO PERON
and to all our French and Argentine friends
who helped us to succeed

to

the ARGENTINE DOCTORS
who restored us to fight another day

to

our RELATIVES who
encouraged us to start.

PREFACE

IT was my intention to write an account on my own of the expedition to Aconcagua, if I returned; but an attack of lumbago prevented me from participating in the second part of the ascent. Consequently I enlisted the help of Guy Poulet, who took part in the final attack on the summit, to take up the narrative where I was forced to abandon it. I have every reason to be pleased with the assistance he rendered me, and I am convinced that the reader will be equally satisfied.

The publication of this account was also helped by the diaries and memoranda of Lucien Berardini, Adrien Dagory, Edmond Denis, Pierre Lesueur and Robert Paragot, so that this book can be regarded to some extent as the work of the whole team.

RÉNÉ FERLET.

CONTENTS

PART ONE:

THE APPROACH by Réné Ferlet

PART TWO:

THE ASSAULT by Guy Poulet

CONTENTS

ILLUSTRATIONS

MAPS AND DIAGRAMS

PART ONE: THE APPROACH

by Réné Ferlet

Chapter One

IN SEARCH OF ADVENTURE

February 1952

AFTER a struggle lasting for several weeks, the first
French expedition to the Argentine Andes ended
in triumph. (*Translator's Note:* Réné Ferlet was
a member of this expedition.) On February 2nd,
Guido Magnone and Lionel Terray reached the summit
of Fitz-Roy, the impregnable bastion of stormy Patagonia, after two days' epic fight against almost incessant
bad weather, with new snow up to their waists and a
furious gale ever blowing straight in from the Antarctic,
which forced them to go to ground like beasts of the field
in forests and in the snow.

We therefore accepted with pleasure a proposal from
our Argentine liaison officer, Francisco Ibanez, to make
an attempt on Aconcagua. His description of the Central
Andes, coupled with the promise of a better climate,
removed the last scruples of the partisans for a reconnaissance to Cerre Torre, so we decided to go. After an
enthusiastic reception at Buenos Aires, we flew on to
Mendoza. It was early March and the weather was
wonderful—just being able to go about in shirt-sleeves
was enough to make us happy.

We drew up our plan of attack at Puente del Inca.
The ordinary route up Aconcagua, a stony track well
supplied with huts, did not seem to us to be worthy of
the conquerors of Fitz-Roy. We therefore decided to try
the South Arête,* an interesting route in that it would

* The explanation of this and similar technical terms will be found
in the Glossary at the end of the book.

3

permit us to examine from close to the formidable problem of the South Face of the mountain. From the shores of Lake Horcones, half an hour above the military refuge of Puente del Inca, the huge wall, enormous in spite of the distance, and crowned by the two summits of the highest mountain in the Americas, was visible far away at the end of the valley. Not all the Face was visible from this view-point—only the top part, perhaps 1,000 metres or so, could be seen. Who knew what the lower 2,000 metres might hold in store for us, hidden as they were by the peaks of Almacen and Mirador?

Quietly jogging along on my mule, I pondered over the ascent. One did not need to be a great mountaineer to visualise the importance of the task before us. With the aid of my field-glasses I climbed the icy spurs and ascended couloirs. This preliminary study led me to the conclusion which I already anticipated. In order to attempt this climb with any chance of success it would be necessary to have at our disposal a very strong party both from the standpoint of technique and morale, combined with luck and two months of summer weather, which latter were now no longer possible. This rapid survey put paid to any immediate hope that I had of making an attempt, but even as I abandoned the idea I promised myself to return later. As our time was very short, our attempt on the South Arête was limited to a reconnaissance as far as the first of the major difficulties, and, like our predecessors, we climbed Aconcagua by the ordinary route.

October 1953

"Can you take three or four months' holiday?"

Somewhat surprised by my question, Robert Paragot quickly realised that it could mean only one thing—going on an expedition, and with quickened interest replied:

"Certainly. Where are we going?"

4

"To climb the South Face of Aconcagua."

It will be noticed that I was no longer talking of an attempt, so certain was I of success if I could but get together the party which I had had in mind for some time.

"The only thing is that you will have to put 100,000 francs [£100] in the kitty."

"I'll find them. When do you want them?"

He looked depressed for a moment, and then brightened up when he realised that he could have a month in which to find the money. I knew that another question was on the tip of his tongue, so, to put him out of his misery, I explained that I was waiting for Lucien Berardini, to ask him to take part also. Having seen both these men in action, I knew their worth and their high morale. They were young—Robert was twenty-seven and Lucien twenty-three—and both had excellent records: such as the West Face of the Dru, Pointe Walker, on the North Face of the Grandes Jorasses, West Face of Mont Mallet, East Face of the Grand Capucin and many other expeditions, where these two bright young men, raised in the most difficult school of rock-climbing, always either climbed together or each leading his own rope.

A broad smile spread over the bronzed visage of Lucien as he listened to me, and, with the enthusiasm characteristic of him, he there and then undertook to attempt the impossible.

As for me, now assured of the participation of the best possible French "rope", I felt ready to give a detailed exposition of my plans. We both agreed to ask our friend Adrien Dagory to undertake the cinematography of the expedition, as George Strouvé was not available. Adrien, who was a little over thirty, was a resourceful chap in a variety of ways. By profession a chocolate manufacturer, he was much more drawn towards adventure in any form than the manufacture of sweets. Photography was his passion, and he was also an enthusiastic flyer. Although he held a civil and also glider pilot's licence, he had found time to take up climbing seriously. In fact he was a first-rate climber, and had taken part in the first ascent of the West Face of the Dru, and moreover—a rare phenomenon in a climber—he was a determined character. This quality was of great advantage for an expedition, and I knew that Didi, as he was invariably called at the French climbing school at Fontainebleau, was always the one who exercised a calming influence in moments of crisis. He had dreamed for years of setting out on a far-off mountain expedition. When I rang him up he accepted immediately, and I knew from the quickening in his voice how happy he was to be able to do so.

Next day we all met in my office and made a careful examination of the only valid piece of documentary evidence in our possession—a very bad photograph of the South Face given to me in 1952 by my Andean friend, Alfredo Magnani. Despite the lack of detail, we endeavoured to penetrate the mysteries of the great Face and to sum up its difficulties and dangers, for on a wall of these proportions avalanches and stone-fall must play a predominating role. My impression of 1952 was confirmed by this preliminary study and our ensuing discussion—namely, that it would be more than ever necessary to include at least two additional climbers in the party. I had always wished to take my particular climbing friends along with me; in Patagonia, Lionel Terray, Jacques Poincenot and I had been like the Three Musketeers. At that time only bad luck had prevented Guy Poulet from coming with us, and that was why today I at once thought of him.

He left Joinville as a major in 1943 and had just turned thirty. He was a professor of physical culture at the high school of Janson de Sailly, which kept him in good training, in addition to which he was an active sportsman. Mountaineering was his chief passion, which no one knew better than myself, for we had climbed together all over the Alps, accompanied by Jacques Poincenot and the great climber, Pierre Allain. Guy was a likeable fellow, and with his equable disposition would act as a foil to my characteristic hastiness.

While we were searching our brains for a sixth companion, Robert suddenly exclaimed, "We're forgetting 'Lafleur'!" "Lafleur" was Pierre Lesueur, who had been training for a guide's diploma for some months at Chamonix, and in view of the fact that we no longer saw him on Sundays at Fontainebleau, he was automatically listed among those who had disappeared for various reasons, such as marriage, military service and so on. At the age of twenty-seven, he already had a remarkable climbing record, and his last two exploits—first ascents of the North Face of the Grand Dru and of the North Ridge of the Caiman—bore witness to his prowess. In fact we had all known him for so long that his right to be with us was never questioned.

A party of six members split up into three ropes of two is the ideal number for a light expedition, for, as everyone knows, two on a rope forms the most manageable and speedy team on a difficult ascent.

Being anxious to reduce all unforeseen risks to a minimum, I suggested adding an extra member to the party, in case anyone fell out. My proposal was readily accepted, and our choice fell upon Edmond Denis. Although he was only twenty-two years of age, he had already given striking proof of his quality as a climber, and Robert, who was with him on the Pointe Walker, had no need to urge his claim. The list of participants was now complete.

There still remained further problems to be solved, particularly that appertaining to the appointment of an M.O. to the party. It was, of course, necessary to accept certain risks when undertaking an expedition of this nature, for one never knew what might occur, and the possibility of a serious accident must always lurk in the background, so that the presence of an M.O. on an expedition is largely a *sine qua non*. In my opinion, he should also be a surgeon, in order to be able to cope with a really serious accident, the more so because as a rule most expeditions set out to attempt peaks far removed from human habitation. In most cases, too, base camp is some days', if not weeks' journey from civilisation and the resources of a modern hospital.

The situation with regard to Aconcagua was, however, quite different. We would be able to reach the modern hospital of Las Cuevas within six or seven hours at most. We were thus faced with conditions somewhat similar to those met with in the Alps, and after due consideration we decided to dispense with the services of a medical officer. This was really just as well, for it is by no means easy to find a doctor or surgeon who has the necessary time at his disposal, added to which he must possess the requisite qualities of a climber and have a liking for life in lonely places far from the madding crowd. We had, however, two medical chests containing bandages and first-aid kit sufficient for any emergency.

The Second French Expedition to the Argentine Andes therefore consisted of eight persons, seven men and one woman—my wife Suzanne. She was very fluent in Spanish, and would be useful as interpreter to the expedition.

I now had to think of the hundred and one things necessary for an overseas expedition, and here the real work began. The magnitude of this task and the little time left to me to cope with all the difficulties which kept piling up, caused me many sleepless nights. Time was the big factor—it was already October 15th. I never ceased to remember that the "Charles Tellier" would leave Bordeaux on December 18th, and I was alarmed at my audacity in trying to organise alone an enterprise of this nature in so short a time.

As one might guess, the decisive factor was that of finance. It was all the more difficult because, whereas normally one limits the choice of the project to the means at one's disposal, in my case I had to do exactly the opposite—namely, reconcile my scheme with our available means. In most expeditions it is usual to consider Frs. 800,000 (£800) as the minimum personal contribution, but we could not raise more than Frs. 1,500,000 (£1,500) between us, the balance being obtained by loans and advances. This will give some idea of the prodigious economy, guile and financial equilibrium which were necessary in order to make both ends meet. Each and every one of us had not only literally to empty his pockets, but had also to scrape together every penny he could. Adrien pawned his car, and Pierre, who was still in Chamonix, took on the job of porter, which not only got him into training for an expedition in which there were no *sherpas* (there are no porters in Argentina), but also helped him to earn an honest penny by carrying loads up the mountain at Frs. 50 per kilo (6*d*. per pound). For my part, I succeeded in obtaining some money on account from various newspapers for a report to be furnished on our return.

In spite of all our efforts, however, I invariably found myself very restricted from a financial point of view. Fortunately the life of an expedition leader has its lighter moments, and in the course of my peregrinations I encountered sympathetic understanding on the part of most of my suppliers. One day I had the pleasure of being able to tell my friends that the Compagnie Maritime des Chargeurs Réunis was prepared to grant us advantageous terms. At last, after having given up everything which was not absolutely indispensable, we won the day. Provided that we did not incur any outrageous expenditure we could start, and in order to do so we were prepared to accept almost any conditions. For surely this was going to be the most extraordinary alpine venture of all time. It was not our intention to attempt, like our predecessors, to climb a peak of over 7,000 m. and plant the French flag on its summit. Had such been our desire, we would have chosen a virgin peak and climbed it by the easiest route. Our plan was quite different. Sure of our strength and the adequacy of our equipment, we intended to climb our chosen peak by the most difficult route of all.

The reader may well ask, why add to the ordinary risks inherent in the ascent of a great mountain those incurred in a very difficult climb? The answer is quite simply that, as the sport of climbing does not deviate from the general rules, the best climbers try to perfect their art by attempting ascents of ever greater difficulty. I am convinced that no mountaineer, even those who are interested only in bagging peaks or undertaking difficult climbs quite mechanically, can remain unaffected by the golden splendour of a sunrise, the elegance of a narrow ridge of snow mounting towards the heavens or the airy grace of an anemone which has survived, as by a miracle, between two blocks of granite. I can still remember my astonishment at discovering a beautiful miniature alpine garden right in the middle of the famous North Face of Piz Badile.

From the first halting steps, right up to the end of what has been called the "golden age" of mountaineering, which reached its zenith in 1865 with the ascent of the Matterhorn, the aim and object of every climber has been the attainment of a summit. Whymper, Stephens, Tuckett, Kennedy and their contemporaries did not mind how they arrived at the summit of their choice; they all chose the route which seemed to them to be the easiest. The equipment they employed was rudimentary, but sufficient for the climbs in question, most, if not all of which offered more objective dangers than actual tech-

nical difficulty. Although the great majority of the
mountains were as yet unclimbed, there was keen competition among the best climbers to be the first to scale
the finest-looking peaks. When Whymper neared the
top of the Dent Blanche he caught sight of the cairn
erected by Kennedy the year before. Doubtless not wishing to have made only the second ascent of the mountain, he told his guides to turn round and begin the
descent. (*Translator's Note:* This is not quite true:
Kennedy's ascent was made *three* years before, and
Whymper's abrupt *volte face* was not occasioned by pique,
although it would have been entirely in keeping with his
character.)

In the course of this extremely prolific epoch so many
noteworthy ascents were made that it would be impossible to single out any one in particular, with the sole
exception of the conquest of the Matterhorn.

The profound significance of this heroic age did not lie
in its isolated exploits, but in the general result achieved.
At first about nine-tenths of the highest peaks were still
virgin, if not unknown, whereas at the end the majority
had been climbed and a new sport—"Mountaineering"
—had arrived.

Following upon the conquest of the summits (which
were relatively few in number, for Whymper in particular recognised as such only Mont Blanc, the Grandes
Jorasses and the Aiguille Verte, in the whole of the chain
dominating Chamonix and Courmayeur), a new era
opened with the founding of the alpine clubs.

At the start of this second era the majority of climbers
were content to follow the routes already worked out on
the most famous peaks. However, if the main object of
an expedition had previously been that of reaching a
summit by the easiest and quickest possible route, the
more ambitious followers of the new sport no longer
thought of the summit alone, but of the manner of
attaining it. The experts soon discovered that there were

numerous routes bristling with difficulties even on the best-known and easiest of peaks. Thus, ten years after it was thought that the conquest of the Alps was complete, the whole business began all over again.

Legions of mountaineers of a high order, among them A. F. Mummery and Guido Rey, forerunners of modern acrobatic climbing, opened up routes which are still today considered as classic. At the start of the First World War there was not a single important peak which had not been climbed by several routes. At this time began a new technical development—that of guideless climbing—for some of the best climbers of the day had advanced so far as to be able to dispense with the assistance of the formerly indispensable companions of the pioneers.

What may be called the era of modern mountaineering began in 1919. In France, despite four years of war which kept our men away from the mountains, there was an appreciable increase in the membership of the Club Alpin Français, and by the end of 1919 its numbers had reached the respectable total of 5,000. In the same year the "Groupe de Haute Montagne" was formed by Jacques de Lépiney. This academic club started with twenty-six active members. Today the membership of the C.A.F. exceeds 30,000, but of these only 180 have the honour of being active members of the most select climbing club of all, the G.H.M. At the present time the younger generation is turning towards the mountains. In order to understand the spirit which inspires them, let us read what Pierre Dalloz says:

"Dedicated to war, ready to go when duty called, we had been prepared for many months to play our part in action which in our imagination was synonymous with danger and glory. But it was not to be. On a fine and dry November morning the Armistice guns announced to us that we were saved.

Now our abundant energy had to be found an outlet and the mountains fulfilled our urgent need.
Whereas others found solace in business, politics or
pleasure, we surrendered ourselves to them body
and soul. They enabled us to rise to the heights of
our dreams, to prove our valour and permitted us to
savour the exhilarating joy of the heroic life, such
as we might have had in war."

This thirst for battle and victory is the *leitmotiv* of
climbing. Guideless climbing in the main follows a
general rule. Every peak, even including a number of
satellite summits scarcely worthy of the name, had been
climbed by several routes, and only a few great faces still
offered resistance to the increasing number of aspirants
for fresh laurels. Thus the "playground of Europe" was
rapidly becoming exhausted; and although the number
of overseas expeditions began to multiply in proportion,
it became more and more difficult to find suitable terrain
where those seekers of the "first ascent" could satisfy
their aspirations. The general use of artificial aids, such
as pitons and karabiner, which had their origin in the
Eastern Alps, helped Pierre Allain, Ricardo Cassin,
Anderl Heckmair, Guisto Gervasutti and other "giants"
to conquer the last remaining problems one by one. The
death-knell of the invincibility of the great faces was
finally sounded in 1938 by the German success on the
North Face of the Eiger and the Italian ascent of the
Pointe Walker of the Grandes Jorasses. But before long
the Second World War wrote finis to this second "golden
age" of mountaineering.

What is left for those mountaineers of my generation,
who, deprived of climbing during the occupation, wish
now that the war is over to come to grips with the Alps?
Very little. However, if man is unable to create new
mountains, his imagination can at least suggest a remedy.
Competition for the first repetition of the great routes is

now the principal object of the best climbers. The fight against time also plays a part, where one attempts to do in a day what the first-comers accomplished in two. This, however, is merely a phase, and will not last long. Faces, the very names of which were quite enough to terrify most of us a few years ago, have now been climbed twenty times or more. And now—the most recent effort of a sport which will not die—the technique of artificial climbing, pushed to the limit, has made possible the ascent of the West Face of the Dru, regarded as impossible until quite recently. Although there are today still a large number of fine peaks for the climber of average ability who does not wish to try anything new, there is little enough left for those who still seek impressive first ascents.

During the conquest of the Alps, the adventurous side of climbing suffered much from the over-descriptive itineraries so prevalent in modern climbing guides, which abound in descriptions of routes of all grades of difficulty combined with variations of diverse cunning. Actually, given a good sketch-map, the few lines of explanation which generally precede the meticulous description of the routes should be sufficient. In certain specialist guides two pages or more have been devoted to describing the best method of climbing 40 feet of Grade 5 in the Knubel crack on the Grépon. Can it be thought fun, when climbing in one of the mountain chains—now little more than climbing schools—if the leader who is jammed in a crack has to wait while his second rapidly turns over the pages of his guide-book in order to tell him whether the missing hold which will get him out of his predicament is to the right or to the left? The too-prevalent construction of mechanical lifts, the provision of huge barracks, which are still called "refuges", and the tremendous spate of tourists in the mountains during the last few years have hastened the death-knell of a fine sport. The modern climber has no desire to enter huts holding 250 persons, most of whom are tourists hoisted up there by *téléfériques*, where he is often regarded as an intruder and always looked upon as a curious sort of animal. Today the climbing *élite* is faced with two alternatives: either to carry on his sport below the cables which sooner or later will festoon peaks and valleys, accepting as an occupational risk the showering of empty bottles upon his devoted head by the occupants of the tram-cars overhead, or to set off in search of a new Eldorado in far-off mountain chains which have become reasonably accessible by means of modern transport methods. Unfortunately this paradise is closed to most of us on financial grounds.

There are many thousands of virgin peaks among the mountains of the world, but if one is forced to abandon the Alps owing to the lack of new routes, more than one summit is demanded as compensation for the effort of organising an expedition. Moreover, the mountain chains outside Europe are suffering from the effects of technical development.

Many nations have sent their best climbers to the Himalayas since 1947. The usual objective is the conquest of one or more of the fourteen 8,000 m. (26,240 feet) peaks in which the enormous range abounds. After repeated attempts, success was not long delayed, and since the French victory on Annapurna started the ball rolling, Everest, Nanga Parbat and K 2 have been climbed.

Ten more giants still remained unclimbed, but as the height record reached its climax in the ascent of Everest, they have lost a certain amount of their interest from this point of view. Some mountaineers are now striving to attempt the "more difficult" in place of the "ever higher" complex, in that they endeavour to reach the highest summit without employing oxygen or *sherpa* porters.

Roger Duplat, leader of the Lyons climbers, was quite alive to this tendency; and, wishing to avoid the principle of "the summit for the summit's sake", he conceived the idea of combining high-altitude climbing with a high degree of difficulty. In 1952 he started a new line of thought for overseas expeditions by attempting to link up the twin summits of Nanda Devi in the Garhwal Himalaya by traversing a ridge several miles long and over 7,000 m. (22,960 feet) in height. Unfortunately, he and his companion Gilbert Vignes disappeared during this attempt.

But the seed sown by Roger Duplat bore fruit in 1953, for, adopting his idea, I intended to launch the best possible climbing team on an attempt to ascend a 7,000 m. (22,960 feet) peak by the most difficult route. I had no difficulty in finding such a peak: the South Face of Aconcagua.

Chapter Two

THE STRUGGLE FOR THE SUMMIT

THE Andes, a succession of mountain ranges more than 7,000 km. (4,375 miles) in length, is the longest mountain chain in the world. Its first peaks rise in Colombia, near the Caribbean Sea, and in the far south, before tailing off into the frozen wastes of the Antarctic, they leave behind, as a last reminder, the giant ice mountain of Sarmiento, soaring up in the icy solitudes of the island of Tierra del Fuego.

Although since the discovery of the Himalayas the Andes has lost its claim to be the highest range in the world, nevertheless it is one of the highest massifs in existence. Aconcagua, queen of the southern hemisphere, attains the height of 7,035 m. (23,075 feet) above the adjacent waters of the Pacific Ocean, and across the equator a whole multitude of peaks exceeding 6,000 m. (19,680 feet) are scattered abroad in Peru, Bolivia, Chile and Argentina.

The morphology of the various chains, and above all the varying climatic conditions—starting in the Tropics, the Andes pass through the sub-tropical and the southern temperate zones before terminating in the Antarctic—profoundly change the aspect of the mountains. In Bolivia and the extremely dry Argentine provinces of Salta and Jujuy the snow level is not encountered until about 6,000 m. (19,680 feet), which is almost at the top of the highest peaks. Three thousand kilometres (1,880 miles) further south in the Andes of Patagonia, where precipitation, in the form of rain or snow, falls 300 days in the year, the snow level is down to 500 m. (1,640 feet)

17

above sea level. In Colombia and on the Equator the east side of the great peaks which emerge from the huge Amazon forests is covered with an abundant vegetation up to a considerable height. In *la puna*, the altiplano of Chile and North Bolivia, there are immense areas completely bare, stony wastes without trees or even a blade of grass. However, in certain regions, such as San Carlos de Bariloche on Lake Nahuel Huapi, the climate can be favourably compared with that of the Alps. The majority of the mountains forming the chain are of volcanic origin, some of them, separated by great distances, being still active.

Aconcagua, the highest mountain of both American continents, is situated in the heart of the High Andes at about the latitude of Buenos Aires. Rising from a massive base, like most of the Andes peaks, it dominates its neighbours by 1,500 m. (4,920 feet), attaining a height exceeding 7,000 m. (22,960 feet), and is thus the only mountain of this height outside the Asiatic ranges. It is visible from the Pacific, 170 km. (106 miles) distant, and the large Chilean towns of Santiago and Valparaiso are virtually in its shadow. It can be seen from the Trans-Andean Railway and the road from Mendoza to Santiago, a few miles to the north of a great trans-continental air route. It is not only the highest point of the continent, but also the best known and most impressive mountain of all.

Who were the first to admire Aconcagua? Nobody will ever know for certain, but the power of the Incas extended right down the continent, from the time of the legendary Cuzco, and, ascending the valley of Uspallata, reached the base of the Andean giant which they christened Acconcahua or Ackon-Cahuac, made up of the expressions *ackon* (of stone) and *cahuac* (he who watches). It is this name—sentinel of stone—which is still borne today by this guardian of three elements: ocean, sky and pampas.

Miles from human habitation it will never become a place of worship or a holy mountain, and it has never figured in the ancient legends of the Indian tribes, as it is so far removed from any of the crossing points of the Cordilleras. It will be several centuries before this giant of the Andes will really take its place in the history of the exploration of the mountains of the world.

There is little doubt that General Don José de San Martin was the first to come to grips with the mountain. This was in 1817. South America was in process of shaking off the yoke of the Spanish conquerors and Argentine territory was already liberated. The Grand Captain of the Army of the Andes proposed to cross this chain at its highest point in the region of Mercedario, Aconcagua and Tunpungato, and 5,300 men, 10,600 mules and 1,600 horses traversed the passes at a height of 4,000 m. (13,120 feet). Dragging their guns and equipment over endless slopes of scree or frozen snow, whipped by a relentless wind, their throats parched by lack of humidity resulting from the altitude, the soldiers of San Martin successfully overcame all obstacles, but the bodies of 6,300 mules and 1,100 horses lined the route from Uspallata to Chile, bearing silent testimony to the sufferings endured by this amazing army.

First of a long list of prominent personalities who had borne witness to the existence and pre-eminence of Aconcagua in their writings, the celebrated British naturalist Charles Darwin was also in the main responsible for the belief, still current today, that Aconcagua was a volcano.

The Frenchman Pierre Joseph Pissis was commissioned by the Chilean Government to undertake a geological and mineralogical survey of the country; therefore he, together with San Martin and Darwin, were the forerunners of our present knowledge of the area of Aconcagua.

He approached the great mountain anxious to make a

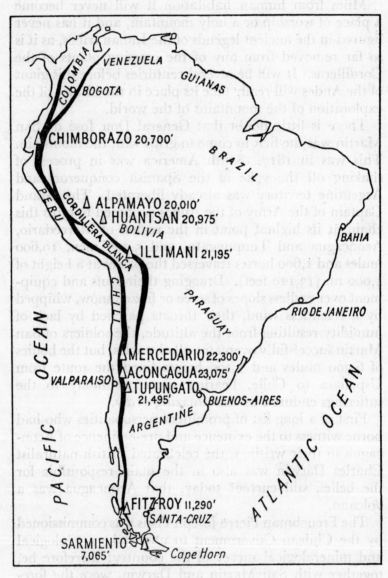

GENERAL MAP OF SOUTH AMERICA, SHOWING THE MOUNTAIN CHAINS
AND THE PRINCIPAL SUMMITS

profound study of the history of its origin. He discovered that it did not possess any of the characteristics
of an active volcano, that its base consisted of sedimentary
rock and that even on the upper slopes of the huge peak
the strata were remarkably regular. The French
mineralogist categorically refused the volcanic origin of
Aconcagua, confirmed its sedimentary structure and
described it as being composed of powerful strata
belonging in all probability to the Triassic and upper
Palæozoic systems. There have been many who followed
in the footsteps of these forerunners and who contributed
much to the knowledge of the massif. Most agreed in
recognising that Aconcagua, although composed in part
of rocks of volcanic origin, had never been a volcano.

Owing to its impressive size—in 1854 it was credited
with a height of 8,610 m. (28,440 feet)—the Stone
Sentinel began to create a definite personality of its own.
In 1883 a man with a will of iron came on the scene, from
far-off Germany—Paul Gussfeldt. He undertook the
tremendous task of climbing the interminable slopes
defending its summit, provided with extremely in-
adequate equipment, and on its eternal snows wrote the
first and most impressive chapter of the history of the
conquest of Aconcagua.

In order to appreciate Gussfeldt's exploit to the full it
must be borne in mind that hitherto little had been
known of this giant of the Andes, it was only very approxi-
mately marked on the existing inaccurate maps of the
period and all that could be seen was a long-distance
view of its West Face. It must be remembered that up to
then the exploration of the range had consisted solely of
the reconnaissance and ascent of a few mountains
situated on the Equator and in Peru. In order to make
an attempt upon it, it was necessary to disregard certain
firmly rooted beliefs emanating from old native legends.

Generally speaking, all ideas on the subject were
essentially vague, and the most ridiculous stories were in

circulation. One school of thought had it that treasures of precious metals were concealed in its slopes, and it was precisely this belief which enabled Gussfeldt to find companions for his venture. For there is little doubt that the few Chilean *arrieros* with no mountaineering experience who accompanied him were filled with the notion of finding gold rather than inspired by the glory of standing upon the summit. Early in February 1883 the German climber left Santiago. It was a long and arduous route to Aconcagua, but nothing deterred him, and entirely lacking in adequate equipment, he launched two bold assaults on the summit. The first one was the most successful, and took him to a height of 6,560 m. (21,480 feet). Only a few hundred feet separated him from the coveted summit, but his porters deserted, and he was forced to beat a retreat and abandon the unequal struggle. His success, however, consisted in having blazed the trail for the party which fourteen years later followed in his tracks and conquered the giant.

It was early in December 1896, the southern summer had not begun and the Andes were still wearing their white winter mantle. The excitement was great at Vacas, a post-stage on the road from Argentina to Chile. This little wooden hut—the only building for miles round—was the starting-point of an important expedition under the leadership of the well-known English climber, Edward Fitzgerald.

He was accompanied by another British climber, Stuart Vines, younger but more experienced, and a team of Swiss and Italian guides led by the already famous Mathias Zurbriggen. Fitzgerald wanted a very strong party, and he had furnished it with ample and carefully chosen equipment. This was just as well, for Aconcagua soon revealed itself as one of the toughest and most ruthless adversaries which climbers of that era had ever had the temerity to attack. Their first task, and by no means the least, was to force the maze which defended the base of the peak. After a reconnaissance up the valley of Rio de las Vacas, Fitzgerald came to the conclusion that it would be worse than useless making the attempt from this side. He therefore transferred his base of operations to Puente del Inca and regrouped his team. On December 18th Zurbriggen, accompanied by an *arriero*, set off to reconnoitre the Horcones Valley with a view to finding a site for an intermediary camp and to locate Aconcagua. The sun blazed down from out of a cloudless deep blue sky, and the burning wind raised clouds of dust from the disintegrated rocks which dried up the throat. Hardly noticing their fatigue, the two men struggled onwards, when suddenly the huge peak reared up before them. After having carefully surveyed the top part of the mountain, Zurbriggen realised that he had come to the foot of the South Face of Aconcagua.

There was no hope from the west and still less from the south. By no means disheartened, the indefatigable Zurbriggen retraced his steps and rejoined the *arriero* at Confluencia. They then turned north up the main Horcones Valley. Darkness fell while they were still under way, so they quickly put up a tent and retired for the night. At dawn Zurbriggen sent back the *arriero* and continued alone up the dreadful valley, and ten hours later he reached the foot of the mountain (at Plaza de Mulas?, 4,200 m., 13,115 feet). Zurbriggen returned to the tent, where he passed a second night, and next morning went up again towards the heights. Leaving his horse at the point where he had turned back the evening before, he began to ascend the huge scree slope which mounts towards the summit. The stones slid away under his feet, and it was not until after several hours of thankless slogging that he reached the height of 5,700 m. (18,700 feet), where, without knowing it, he joined Gussfeldt's route. He made a careful examination of the rest

23

of the route and returned to where he had left his horse. Once more he passed through this repulsive valley, when suddenly his horse stumbled and fell into the gorge, injuring itself severely. Riding was now, of course, out of the question so, continuing the interminable descent on foot, he was overtaken by night, and had to bivouac in the open, numbed by an icy wind. Finally on the 21st he got to the tent, but his strength failed and he was obliged to rest until next day. At Lake Horcones he was met by Stuart Vines and the *arriero*, who had given him up for lost.

Fitzgerald was doubly pleased by the good news, for the very day that Zurbriggen started out on his reconnaissance he learned that the German Athletic Club of Santiago was about to send out an expedition by Gussfeldt's route.

Spurred on by this competition, they decided to attack without delay. Base Camp was set up on December 23rd at 4,270 m. (14,000 feet).

Fitzgerald decided to push on for the summit the same day. Five men set out with food and equipment, but when night came they had not got above 4,870 m. (15,975 feet). They were so tired that darkness fell before they could erect their tents, and they passed a terrible night in the open. When dawn came the five men were in a deplorable condition, two turned back, while the rest feverishly recommenced the ascent. Step by step they toiled up the apparently endless shifting scree, until about midday Fitzgerald realised that it was impossible to go on. Having no wish to undergo the tortures of another night in the open, they prepared a camp. Lochmatter, by now completely exhausted, went back to Base Camp, leaving only Fitzgerald and Zurbriggen to pass their second night on the mountain. (*Translator's Note:* Lochmatter, a member of Fitzgerald's party, came from a famous family of guides living in the Zermatt Valley, Switzerland.) Next day, after they had eaten a little food, the weather deteriorated, so that they were unable to go on. Towards evening, however, it improved, and having made up their minds to fight to a finish, the two men continued the impossible climb. Two hours later, at about 5,800 m. (19,025 feet), a storm was brewing, and Fitzgerald had reached exhaustion point. The retreat was on. Assailed by furious squalls, the two reached Base Camp just as porters arrived from Puente del Inca bearing fresh provisions. After a good meal the main body set off on the 26th to make a bivouac at 5,800 m. (19,125 feet) (Condor's Nest?), while Zurbriggen went on alone to reconnoitre the route. After clambering up the interminable scree for many hours he suddenly came upon a cairn, inside which he discovered a visiting-card left by Gussfeldt fourteen years before. The card bore the following terse statement: "Second attempt on Aconcagua—March 1883". This cairn marked the highest point reached by Zurbriggen, who turned back and went down to rejoin his companions. Next day the whole party assembled in Base Camp to reorganise and prepare a new attack. The second attempt was not destined to get them much higher up the mountain. After a few days' further effort they succeeded in establishing a bivouac at the height of 5,800 m. (19,125 feet). At dawn on New Year's Eve the temperature was −15° C., so they started again up the disintegrated rock and the unstable scree slopes. Hardly had they left their camp than the weather changed once more. To add to their difficulties, a pitiless wind scourged them, growing colder and more furious with every step up the steep slope. They struggled on until at last Zurbriggen, the tough Swiss guide, collapsed with badly frozen feet. Vigorous rubbing partially restored the circulation, but once again they were forced with more difficulty than ever to beat a retreat.

Next day the weather was fine and Zurbriggen felt better, but the party set off without him, Fitzgerald leading. Again they were defeated, but they managed to get within sight of the summit before being compelled to return to Puente del Inca for rest and replenishment of stores. They had passed the extreme point reached by Gussfeldt at about 6,600 m. (21,650 feet).

Aconcagua had now beaten them twice, and they had drunk to the dregs the bitter draught of failure. Thinking that their luck must at last turn, they set off yet once again.

The night of January 10th found them huddled together in the Condor's Nest. At the first light of day, Fitzgerald, Zurbriggen and Pollinger started off on their crusade. At about 6,000 m. (19,680 feet) Fitzgerald collapsed, suffering from violent sickness. Having one hand half frozen, he gave up and turned back, assisted by Pollinger, leaving Zurbriggen alone on the terrible mountain. Avoiding the worst pitches of loose rock and detritus, he eventually reached the summit ridge. Great was his disappointment when he discovered that what he had taken for the summit was nothing more than a mere bump on the ridge. The real summit of Aconcagua lay a considerable distance to the east, and much higher. Still not disheartened, he advanced slowly towards the coveted summit, but his strength gave out and as night fell he returned to camp, in almost as sorry a state as Fitzgerald.

Next day they tried again. This was the fourth time! Would they win through or not? The answer was no, for at 6,400 m. (21,090 feet) Fitzgerald fell, injuring himself, so that they were again forced to retreat. After a "rest day" at 5,800 m. (19,025 feet), Fitzgerald, Zurbriggen, Pollinger and Lanti got ready for what must be the final attempt, for they were determined at all costs to conquer this terrible mountain. Once more they started up the grim track which they had made through the shifting scree. Their progress became slower the nearer they approached the summit. Exhausted—who would not be?—by six weeks of incessant effort, Fitzgerald sank

26

down after a short rest at 6,700 m. (21,975 feet). In vain
he endeavoured to struggle to his feet, but he was completely exhausted. This man with a will of iron had
found his master. He ordered Zurbriggen to go on alone,
and, a wreck of his former self, turned back with Pollinger
and Lanti.

Once again, for the third time, Zurbriggen found himself alone on the mountain. Jaded with fatigue, he
tenaciously continued the climb foot by foot, and suddenly he was there; the miracle was performed! There
was nothing above him; the southern hemisphere and the
two Americas were at his feet.

A cairn and an ice-axe erected on the summit remained
as mute witnesses of the first victory of man over the
Stone Sentinel of the Incas.

Between 1897 and 1946 more than fifty expeditions
made assaults on the mountain, all but one utilising the
now classic route or nearby variations. Climbers from a
large number of nations took part in the attacks, thus
transforming the highest point of the Andes into an
international peak.

A mountain which has been climbed has naturally less
terrors in store than one which is still virgin, consequently none of these later ascents can be compared to
that epic of Fitzgerald's expedition. Nevertheless Aconcagua still remains a very long, laborious and dangerous
climb.

In 1946 an Argentine expedition constructed two
wooden huts on the normal route. The first and largest
was put up at Plaza de Mulas, at 4,200 m. (17,775 feet)
on the site of the usual expedition base camps. The
second, which was in the form of a small tent, was
erected at about 6,200 m. (20,335 feet). It bears the
name of Nicolas Plantamura, the first Argentine to reach
the top.

From this time on the number of expeditions increased

considerably, and every year dozens of climbers essay the ascent of the mountain.

In 1951 two further refuges were added, one, "Eva Peron", is double the size of Plantamura, which is now too small, and the other, "Juan Peron", at 6,600 m. (21,660 feet) is the highest permanent structure in the world.

Today the normal route up Aconcagua is well equipped with huts and can be climbed on mule-back up to a height of 6,750 m. (22,140 feet), so the climb can scarcely be classed as a great ascent. This denigration of the classic route is the common fate of all mountains, and only the discovery of new routes will restore the reputation of a mountain too often climbed.

Chapter Three
THE SEARCH FOR NEW ROUTES

THE highest crest of the Andes bears two summits joined by an easy ridge of about 5,250 feet. The principal summit lies to the north, while to the south the other peak rises to a height of 22,730 feet. The routes up both peaks are identical except for a few hundred feet. That leading to the southern summit is no more difficult than the other, but the attraction of the greater height drew the climbers, and it was not until 1927 that the Englishman, M. F. Ryan, who had already reached the highest point, attempted the South Peak. His attempt failed, and it was left to a German party to stand on the summit snows in 1947—exactly fifty years after Mathias Zurbriggen's victory.

The year 1934 will be known as that in which the first entirely new route was worked out. This time it was a Polish party from the High Tatra which got together the strongest Andean expedition and prepared for a long campaign.

February 24th 1934

The Poles entered the Quebrada Relincho by the valley of Rio de las Vacas, and established an important base camp at the foot of the East Face of Aconcagua.

On March 5th the eternal silence of this lost valley was broken by the preparations for the great ascent. At 15,910 feet the slope became so steep that further progress on muleback was impossible. The climbers split up into three ropes of two men and continued until night overtook them at 18,040 feet. Here they set up their first high camp. Next day they lost several hours seeking for the best way up the mountain. This was completely hidden behind a huge rock cliff. A thorough reconnaissance was now necessary, in order to thread a way up the buttresses and couloirs, so that by the end of the day they had got no higher than 19,355 feet. The cliff was ascended on the 7th, and continuing, the party mounted a very steep glacier. Here the going was laborious, with a strong and icy wind. At 20,665 feet two ropes stopped, and erected their tents on a tiny shelf on the glacier. It was bitterly cold and the thermometer showed 5° F. This was Camp III. Next day, carrying light loads, Dorwaski and Karpinski went on towards the summit, but the hour of victory had not yet come, and they were soon compelled to turn back and go down to Camp II.

The fourth day dawned full of promise. The weather seemed good, for the wind—always a deadly enemy of the climber—had died away, and only a light breeze caressed the desolate slopes of Aconcagua. The cold, however, was still intense when Daszyinski and Osiecki, with Narkiewicz and Ostrowski, started off once more. They had only 2,300 feet to go to reach the top, but, as usual, the last few feet were the most troublesome. The advance slowed down, their feet, shod with crampons, got heavier and heavier, and it was not until the end of the afternoon, after eight hours of strenuous effort, that they were able to complete the conquest of the East Face of Aconcagua.

In 1948 the Swiss climber, Frédéric Marmillod, was coming down the ordinary route. In fifteen years' wandering in South America he had acquired a good working knowledge of the Andes, but the mountains of the Central Cordilleras had made him homesick for his native peaks. While mechanically plodding down the well-beaten mule-track, he dreamed of fine snow arêtes soaring towards the skies. His wish to experience once again the joys of alpine climbing led him, quite naturally, to think of ascending the West Face and South Ridge of Aconcagua.

February 1952

Conditions were bad, the mountain was entirely covered with a thick layer of fresh snow and the weather was unsettled. Consequently Frédéric Marmillod, Dorly —his wife—and Miguel Ruedin could not start out on a big climb; they contented themselves therefore with going up the normal route.

March 1952

The first French Andes expedition had just climbed Fitz-Roy. They were now on the point of leaving Buenos Aires en route for Aconcagua. In their plan, at first rather loosely drawn up, they had now decided on the South Arête. The party, which included Marmillod, had only time to reconnoitre a track practicable for mules, to the foot of the first difficulties of the West Face.

January 18th 1953

Marmillod and his wife met F. Grajales and Lieutenant Francisco Ibanez, who had just come down from his fifth ascent of the mountain, at Plaza de Mulas. The sun had barely risen when the caravan started up the first scree-slopes of the West Face. Although the climbers had spent an entire day beforehand in cutting a track for the mules with their axes, the lower part of the route, which was slashed by a deep gorge, proved very difficult for the animals. Towards four o'clock in the afternoon, at a height of about 19,950 feet, the mules were unable to go any farther, so camp was pitched at the foot of an impressive rock bastion.

The next day was spent in reconnaissance, and it was not until the morning of the 20th that the real ascent began. The weather was good despite a very cold wind which blew from the north-west in violent squalls. Threading their way along the steep scree slope at the foot of the wall towering above them, the climbers reached the bottom of the great couloir which bisects the West Face. This enormous rock gully is the key to the ascent, but in order to reach its foot it is necessary first to ascend a very steep rock wall, about 300 feet high, which completely cuts off the base of the mountain. It appeared possible to surmount it in direct line with the couloir—in fact they had actually climbed part of it the evening before—but in order to husband their strength they proposed today to look for an easier means of access. At last, close to the South Arête, they found a deep and narrow gully full of snow and ice, which enabled them to reach the base of the first large gendârme on the arête at a height of about 19,680 feet. The rock, however, was conglomerate, very crumbly and quite unclimbable. They were obliged to descend about 650 feet to where an easy ledge led them to the foot of the great couloir. This long detour, however, had consumed much time, so that, in view of the somewhat late hour, the four climbers decided to bivouac where they were, under a projecting rock at a height of 18,695 feet.

Next day, having overcome the difficulties of the great couloir, which in places consisted of bare ice between vertical walls, they made a second bivouac at 20,990 feet.

During the night the storm broke, and snow and hail gradually percolated into the sleeping-sacks. When dawn came the weather was still uncertain. They had to break through a thick layer of ice before they could get out of their sacks. To continue the climb was out of the question, so they resigned themselves to wait another day before deciding what to do. Fortunately the weather improved towards evening and, fortified by the sight of a good sunset, they braced themselves to pass their fifth night on the mountain.

They left at 7.30 on the morning of the 23rd under a clear sky, still contending with a very strong and icy wind. Finally, by way of the upper part of the West Face, they reached the South Arête at about 21,975 feet. The sun was shining from a cloudless sky and the wind was gradually dying away. At last luck had intervened and provided them with a magnificent day for their victory. The view from this airy crest was very extensive in all directions. The peaks and glaciers of the Central Andes from Mercedario to Tupungato were spread out before them; to the left sparkled the immense blue expanse of the Pacific, while to the right, almost invisible through the heat haze, lay the vast extent of the Argentine pampas.

This ended the exploration of Aconcagua. What of the South Face? So far no serious attempt had been made upon it. The very sight of this wall of 9,800 feet, rising abruptly from the depths of the Lower Horcones Valley, was enough to instil doubt and terror into the heart of anybody who had dared to venture thus far. There were many who had got as far as its foot—easy up to that point—but they all turned away and "did" the ordinary ascent.

Chapter Four

THE APPROACH

THE "Charles Tellier" had hardly tied up to Argentine territory before we became the prey of a swarm of well-meaning but completely frenzied individuals armed with every type of photographic apparatus. Pulled in all directions, grasped by outstretched hands, we were obliged to make pose after pose, while all the time we were blinded by modern electronic flash-bulbs and deafened by loud explosions, usually accompanied by a cloud of evil-smelling magnesium fumes. However, everything comes to an end, even films and fountain-pen ink, so, having completely exhausted the munitions of war, the gentlemen of the Press left us to our own devices. We took leave of the Captain and ship's officers amidst a bustling crowd of overloaded porters. Once on land, we were at last able to greet the friends who had come to meet us. This blessed respite was unfortunately of short duration, for we had to get our baggage—a mountain of baggage (we had a woman with us!)—through the Customs. We were assisted in this complex operation by Jean Leroy, the obliging Argentine director of the Tourist Office, and André Tunis, head of the Press Office of the French Embassy, so that half an hour later we had really entered Argentina.

It was as much as we could do to cram all our belongings into the two large American cars, kindly provided by the directors of the Motor Club, who were our hosts during our stay in Buenos Aires. Passing along the wide and beautiful Avenue General Peron, we crossed the

Park of Palermo and made for the suburb of Le Tigre, about twenty miles distant.

Ahead of us, driving himself in a luxurious open coupé, was a man in a white linen cap who responded to the *'vivas'* from passers-by with a wave of the hand. This intrigued us, so we put on speed in order to pass him, but when we drew level we greeted him in our turn, for it was none other than General Peron himself, returning to his house at Olivos, entirely without escort of any kind.

We had thought now that we were out of the city we would get a certain amount of peace and quiet, but scarcely had we finished dinner than another horde of pressmen arrived. Eventually we got rid of them and went to bed—but not to sleep. We had reckoned without the mosquitoes, which plagued us all night. Next morning I returned to the customs house, where I found the customs officials doing their best to open our boxes with hammer and chisel. Nothing that I said would stop them until I showed the telegram sent to me before our departure from France by Peron himself. Eventually I had all the boxes transferred to an empty classroom of the Institut Français.

Now I was free to prepare a plan of campaign, and went into conference with R. L. Hauthal and J. F. Fino, respectively President and Secretary-General of the Argentine Ski Federation. These men gave me inestimable assistance in my task.

At the War Office I was very pleased to resume my acquaintance with Major Blanco, who acted as liaison officer between the Army and Andean expeditions. We had met before at Uspallata in 1952 when I was on my way to Aconcagua for the first time. Since the ascent of Fitz-Roy he had come to recognise the efficiency of French climbers, but he also knew Aconcagua. When I spoke of the South Face, I saw in his eyes a look of scepticism, which I was to encounter elsewhere later on. He said that the liaison officer who would accompany us had not yet been appointed, but that there would be no difficulty on that score, apart from choosing someone suitable from among the many applicants. Now that I was assured of the help of the Army for the transport of our equipment from Puente del Inca to our future base camp, a great weight was lifted from my mind.

The next few days were a constant whirl of cocktail parties, official dinners and Press interviews. Ultimately we became so well known that more than once we heard on the street whispers of "French climbers. . . . South Face of Aconcagua."

While I was making feverish preparations for our coming departure for Mendoza, my companions spent their time exploring the largest city of the South American Continent—Buenos Aires.

On January 13th I received a telephone communication to the effect that General Peron had granted my request and that he would receive the French expedition at the Casa Rosada.

He greeted us with great cordiality, and the reception lasted much longer than is usually the case. Peron, who is a skier and climber and former colonel of the Mountain Troops, did not conceal his intense interest in anything appertaining to mountaineering. He was out to do all he could to assist the expedition to attain its objective, and it would have needed little inducement for him to have accompanied us. First of all he made arrangements for a military aircraft to transport the party and all equipment to Mendoza and, knowing that we would like to have a close look at the South Face, he agreed to allow us the use of the plane long enough to make a reconnaissance flight around it. Furthermore, Army mules and trucks would be supplied to convey everything from Mendoza to Base Camp. As soon as we had chosen the site for this camp, a permanent hut would be erected there, which we proposed, with his approval, to name after Jacques Poincenot, our comrade who died in 1952

SCREE SLOPES IN THE UPPER HORCONES VALLEY ON THE WAY UP TO PLAZA
DE MULAS, BASE CAMP FOR THE ORDINARY ROUTE UP THE NORTH FACE OF
ACONCAGUA

A HUGE AVALANCHE SWEEPS THE CENTRAL COULOIR

on the approach march to Fitz-Roy. Expressing anxiety as to how we intended to surmount the sércas of the upper glacier—the principal obstacle on the Face—he suggested a revolutionary solution; namely, that the Air Force should bomb it! This idea pleased him so much that I had great difficulty in dissuading him.

Shortly before our departure I was informed that First Lieutenant Atilio Ramazzi had been appointed as liaison officer. We were to meet him at Puente del Inca, the real starting point of the expedition, and the headquarters of the company of Mountain Skiers which he commanded.

At about 7 a.m. a small jeep brought us all, together with our twenty suitcases, to the Palermo Airport, where we found an Argentine Air Force Dakota awaiting us on the tarmac. It was already loaded up with our two tons of equipment, and after farewells we got aboard and taxied down the runway. Owing to the great weight, our take-off was a little difficult. Our under-carriage had scarcely retracted before we were over the pampas which stretched away for hundreds of miles ahead of us. There seemed no end to it—just a gigantic patchwork of cultivated fields, crops and vast prairies where countless cows were peacefully grazing. Gradually and almost imperceptibly the cultivated land changed to a desert-like steppe with sand dunes and isolated clumps of stunted shrubs. We were now very close to the Andes, but they were hidden behind a thick curtain of cloud, so that Aconcagua remained invisible. In a few moments we made a somewhat bumpy landing on the concrete runway of Mendoza, one of the prettiest towns in Argentina, a veritable oasis at the foot of barren mountains.

We had had a fine trip, and now submitted with good grace to the eternal questionings of the Press. Once again I had to try to explain why we chose to make an attempt on the South Face when there was a perfectly good way up by the normal route. While the Army was busy with our equipment I had a chat with our pilot, Captain Nunez Sanchez, and arranged for a flight round the mountain—atmospheric conditions permitting —very early next morning, before the heat could cause too many air-pockets. We were taken to the officers' mess of the 'Mountain Group of Cuyo' for lunch. Captain Ignacio R. Nazar of this Group was an Aconcagua veteran. In the course of a military expedition to the mountain in 1945 he sustained severe frostbite, necessitating the amputation of half his left foot. Although slightly sceptical of our chances on the South Face, he agreed to do everything possible to facilitate our success.

It was already January 16th, and—fortunately for us— the southern summer, which had started three weeks before, was late. Weather conditions were bad, it seemed, and there were frequent falls of snow down to the 13,100-foot level, so despite our long stay in Buenos Aires we had not lost time. Nevertheless we could not afford to wait any longer if we were to be settled in our Base Camp by January 22nd, as intended. Hoping that conditions would permit a flight round the mountain within the next two days, I fixed January 22nd as a deadline for our departure. That evening Sanchez rang me up and told me that the met. men had predicted first-class conditions for the following morning.

I awoke at the first light of dawn. It was a wonderful day, and even the foothills were clear of their usual morning mist. Fully expecting a bumpy flight, I insisted that Suzanne, who normally did not eat anything early, should have a good breakfast. The Dakota was awaiting us at the airfield, and the two pilots were rather intrigued at the novel mission. To enable us to film and take photographs at our ease, we removed the door and tied ropes across the open space to prevent us from falling out. After a preliminary warming up, the plane, given full throttle, leaped upwards, and we were soon circling above Mendoza. The pilot, who did not really know one mountain from another, first of all took us close to Tupungato, but when we pointed out the error, he turned away to the north, and before long we were 16,000 feet above the Andes, which looked like a frozen sea below us. Suddenly an enormous peak appeared on the horizon. There was no mistaking the huge menacing wall—this was it: Aconcagua South Face was in sight! Immediately we recognised it, tremendous activity broke out, photographers and ciné operators literally fighting for the best positions near the open door. Everyone was tied on to a rope attached to the aircraft, as we did not wish to lose any member of the party at this early stage. As soon as we reached 19,700 feet we flew across the Face at a distance of about a mile. Until now nobody had examined this wall with the express intention of climbing it, and I must say that what we saw would not have inspired anybody to do so, unless, like us, they had been preparing for it for months.

I endeavoured to concentrate on the route chosen from the photograph, and just as I had located the central buttress, an avalanche of gigantic proportions swept down, hiding the lower part of the Face behind a cloud of snow resembling an atomic explosion. The snow-cloud had not cleared away before another avalanche, even larger than the first, came down from another direction. It seemed as though the mountain was throwing down a challenge by revealing its most powerful defences. We now turned for a second crossing and went up to our ceiling of about 20,300 feet. The aircraft began to oscillate violently, and our ears hummed. Lucien and Edmond took oxygen, and Suzanne was not feeling at all well. On the other hand, the photographers, busy at their job, did not seem to be affected. This time I concentrated on the séracs of the upper glacier, which were said to form the crux of the climb. The plane vibrated continuously the whole time, but not sufficient to prevent me observing that the séracs seemed lower and less steep above the central buttress than elsewhere. If this was actually the case, the greatest problem of the Face was solved and the ascent was possible. However, before counting our chickens, I wanted to make absolutely certain. We had crossed the Face at a distance of about 4,900 feet, so that it was possible that I had made a mistake, for owing to the vibration I could not use field-glasses, therefore another and closer crossing was essential.

I made my way along to the pilot's seat, pausing to reassure Suzanne, who wanted to go back, as, despite her flying-suit she was suffering from the cold. Since my flight over Fitz-Roy in Patagonia, when the aircraft, in a wind of about 110 miles per hour, suddenly dropped about 50 feet without any dire results, my confidence in Argentine pilots and Dakotas remained unshaken. However, this must definitely be the last crossing of the Face. Above the noise of the engines I shouted to the pilot in my best Spanish: "*Yo quiero hacer una otra vuelta. Pero, esta vez, el mas cerca que se puede de la pared*" (I should like to make another crossing, but this time as near as possible).

"*Muy bien, Señor*" (With pleasure, Monsieur), he replied, as though it was the easiest thing in the world.

I added, hastily, "*Sin demasiado peligro*" (Don't take risks!)

His reply was lost in the noise of the engines, increased to full throttle, and the vibration of the plane as we turned sharply away. From this manœuvre and an upward gesture of his thumb, I knew that my request had been understood.

The view from the pilot's cockpit was much more extensive than from the rear of the aircraft. The whole of the massif from Mercedario to Tupungato—an upheaval of enormous peaks crushed as though in some gigantic cataclysm—lay spread out before us. Straight ahead was Aconcagua, easily the highest of this group of snow-wreathed giants. Large white clouds like cauliflowers floated above the plain, and some of them were beginning to penetrate the lower valleys. After a few minutes I noticed that we were not gaining height, and realised that we had reached our maximum ceiling, which, after a hasty calculation—why does not everybody use the metric system?—I made out to be about 21,400 feet. Aconcagua was rapidly approaching, and it appeared as though we must crash into the mountainside unless we changed course, when suddenly we swept up over the middle of the South Arête not more than 650 feet from the face. We seemed to be right on top of the upper glacier, and the huge séracs, as large as houses, and piled one upon the other, looked so close that I began to be a little alarmed at the audacity of the pilot. In spite of our speed, I was able to confirm my first impression that this ice-cliff would "go". I should have liked to have a look at the upper slopes of the mountain, but very strong air currents made the plane vibrate so much that that was impossible. I signed to the pilots that the job was done, and returned to the freezing fuselage. My wife, who was still green with fear, soon perked up when she saw that we were going down, and Lucien and Edmond were equally glad. On the other hand, Adrien was in his element. He had been able to satisfy his two passions: cinematography and flying. Guy and Robert had also taken scores of photographs, so that between us we ought to have some excellent pictures of the Face.

We exchanged impressions. Terrifying in its size, the Face was undoubtedly very steep. The top two-thirds were plastered with snow and plentifully supplied with hanging glaciers, whence came the avalanches which seemed to be its most formidable defence. Pierre, who had noticed the bad quality of the rock, added that falling stones were also likely. The lower part of the Face did not appear to present any insuperable difficulty, and as regards the séracs of the upper glacier, we were agreed that they would "go". Taking all in all, we were optimistic. Full of bounce, we had only one wish—to come to grips with our opponent as soon as possible.

January 18th

I called on the commander of the Group at about 9 a.m. After the usual exchange of greetings and the inevitable coffee, he said, "A lorry and command car are at your disposal; you can start when you like."

At long last we were going to leave the plains and strike in to the heart of the Cordilleras. Within a few days we should have gone beyond Puente del Inca and would be setting up our Base Camp. Once there, we could study at leisure the Face we had come so far to see.

"Well, what have you decided?"

"We will leave tomorrow at 7 a.m."

Everybody was delighted when, at the time arranged —an unprecedented miracle—we got into our two vehicles. At first there was a rush for the command car, but the very restricted view from it at once discouraged most of the party, so Suzanne and I remained in sole possession of the comfortable bench seat of this vehicle designed for war rather than for touring. Our friends, preferring to put up with a little discomfort rather than miss the view, crowded on top of the equipment piled up in the lorry. From this dominating position they would obviously enjoy a marvellous view of the Andes, but at the same time would collect all the dust from the track as well.

We soon left Mendoza and its suburbs behind and got on to a wide concrete road skirting the foothills, straight as an arrow for some twenty-five miles. It was a pleasure to drive along it, and in order not to miss anything, I pulled back the canvas cover and, standing with my arms on the top, contemplated the desolate spectacle before me. This huge, arid plain was completely devoid of any sign of vegetation, apart from a few stunted shrubs and the inevitable cacti. Away to the left were still signs of the old Indian trail leading from Mendoza to Uspallata.

A little further on, the road bore to the west and entered the mountains. It was no longer concreted, and our passage raised clouds of dust. At the request of the occupants of the lorry close behind us, we went on ahead, so as not to smother them entirely.

The first zig-zags now began to appear, and our driver took us round the tight curves with ever-increasing zest. The contours changed abruptly. Enormous outcrops and huge bastions of disintegrated rock appeared on all sides. The deeply cut flanks of these hostile mountains were now covered with sparse tufted vegetation, and only the cacti really seemed to take a pleasure in life. They were everywhere, and their huge candles with white stems grew in some cases to a height of over six feet. Bristling with spikes from four to six inches long, they presented a most bizarre appearance—something like an enormous pin-cushion. It is not advisable to come into contact with these spikes, which are so hard that the Indians, after boring a hole through them, use them as needles.

Rounding a bend, we suddenly came upon a little dell through which plashed a little stream surrounded by numerous trees, flowers and well-kept lawns. This oasis of freshness formed a delightful background to the Spa Hotel of Villavicencio.

Bend succeeded bend, and finally we got a last glimpse of the lovely oasis and the red roofs of the spa nestling amid the green leaves far below.

The air was becoming fresh, as we were approaching 8,200 feet, and the cacti were receding. A number of more or less wild horses were grazing the rank yellowish grass. At our approach they kicked up their heels and galloped off. A frightened pampas ostrich crossed the road at full speed. Smaller than its African brother, it is very abundant in this region. Hares, armadillos and lizards completed the local fauna.

We reached the col where the road crossed the foothills of the Andes at a height of 9,840 feet. Before us, as far as the eye could see, lay the enormous extent of the Cordilleras—countless peaks separated by deep valleys, a universe of rocks, scree, plateaux, precipices and rock walls—an incredible chaos. No forests, not even a tree or a bush, broke the monotony of the countryside: it was like a lunar landscape. Above this bristling jumble of limestone mountains could be seen a few snow-tipped peaks. This world of rocks, quite beyond human conception, stretched for hundreds and hundreds of miles, relieved only by an extraordinary medley of the most amazing colours. Deep mauves, reds of every shade, greens, browns, black and white succeeded each other or merged into one another on the walls and in the valleys of this incredible massif.

And there, far above this veritable maze of rocks, soared the summit ridge of Aconcagua, asserting its unquestioned supremacy.

We now descended the other side of the pass towards Uspallata. The driver, doubtless disgruntled at the slow ascent, accelerated more and more. He took all the curves at full speed, apparently without caring what might be coming up. I was extremely apprehensive, for although I was aware that the road was not much used, I trembled to think what fate would befall us if we had the misfortune to meet another vehicle. By an amazing bit of luck the only other car we met was on a straight stretch. At last, to my great relief, the slope eased off and the curves disappeared.

After a few more miles of steppe-like plateau, we reached the village of Uspallata.

44

The presence of water had wrought miracles here. We had suddenly left an arid desert and were plunged into a land of flowers and gardens. Rows of poplars and weeping willows lined the roadside, marking the course of streams running down from the hills. We stopped in a shady avenue and waited for the others to catch us up. When they did so, they were almost unrecognisable under the thick coating of dust from the road. However, after a lot of back-slapping, followed by a quick wash in the stream, they looked nearly human.

Apart from the garrison of mountain troops, Uspallata has only a small population, but the beautiful situation and the healthy climate have encouraged building projects which are now in course of construction. Soon the town will boast 10,000 inhabitants.

We were very courteously received by the C.O., Colonel Agustoni, who knew in advance of our plans and promised to do his best for us.

We took the road again at 5 p.m. We had driven some sixty miles since leaving Mendoza, and still had another fifty to do before reaching Puente del Inca.

No sooner had we left the town behind than the interminable desert began again, and our driver recommenced his special technique of *descente en slalom*. The valley of the River Mendoza opened out before us, and I heaved a sigh of relief as I realised that we were faced with only one more descent worthy of the name. Down this valley flowed all the water from Aconcagua—we were at last on the threshold of the Cordilleras. Enormous slopes of coloured scree rose up on both sides of the valley to the peaks above, 13,100–16,400 feet in height. In spite of their great altitude, these mountains were devoid of snow or ice; nevertheless they were impressive. The road now began the long climb up to Puente del Inca, and on the opposite bank, above a high bluff of alluvial matter washed by the river, the double track of the

45

Transandean Railway was visible, with its bold viaducts and tunnels.

The narrow road, almost entirely without protection on the valley side, was cut out of the rock or built out over the abyss, and once more I could not help wondering what would happen if we met a vehicle coming from the other direction, especially if it was going as fast as we had recently been doing ourselves.

We stopped to fill up with water from a beautiful mountain torrent which was full of trout, and while there we saw a local fisherman catch two or three. After Polvareda—a miserable huddle of huts lining the roadside—the valley widens out as far as Punta de Vacas, where two lateral valleys came in. To the left, over a V-shaped notch, could be seen the snow-cone of Tupungato, the second highest summit of the Andes. On the other side was the opening of the green and narrow gorge of the River of Las Vacas. This was the route taken by Edward Fitzgerald on the occasion of his first reconnaissance of Aconcagua, in 1897.

We continued up the main valley, and a little further on came upon the simple cemetery where rest the many victims of Aconcagua. This corner of Argentine soil was quite international in character, for here lay the remains of Argentine, British, American and Yugoslav citizens and many others.

The end of our long journey was at last in sight, for presently we passed a sign indicating the entrance to Puente del Inca. Our driver stopped before the military refuge. This group of large stone buildings, serving as headquarters for the company of Mountain Skiers, was very different from the usual type of skiers' hut found in the Alps—in fact one of them was three storeys high and was used both as the officers' mess and guest house.

It was almost 8 p.m., and our arrival caused some excitement in this lonely outpost. We were at once surrounded by a mob composed of all ranks, who questioned our drivers incessantly. An officer appeared, the hubbub ceased and I realised that it was the O.C. himself.

"*Teniente Primero Atilio Ramazzi.*"

"*Rene Ferlet, Jefe de la Expedicion.*"

Tall and slender, his smiling face adorned with a short moustache, our liaison officer won our confidence. I felt that he would relieve us of all our worries, and was very glad that he was coming with us.

Atilio could not put us up at the refuge, as the interior was in process of repair, but he had reserved rooms for us at the only hotel in the place. He lived there himself with his young and pretty wife, Ibis. Monsieur Lanatti, the manager, received us in a most friendly manner. Here again our arrival caused a sensation. We at once became the centre of attraction for the hotel guests, though there were not many at this time of year.

After a short rest we went down to dinner. Our table was very lively; in addition to Atilio and Ibis, our party also included Dr. Antinucci and his wife and son. Antinucci, a doctor from Buenos Aires, always spent his holidays at Puente del Inca, where he acted as M.O. for the district for a period of about two months. He was a great admirer of France, and spoke the language fluently. He knew many stories about former expeditions and told them so well that our dinner lasted well into the evening.

When I went to bed, however, the ever-present spirit of Aconcagua took a hold on me and I could not sleep.

Chapter Five

RECONNAISSANCES

Wednesday January 20th

THE sun was shining into the room. Its light was so strong that I easily awoke from a restless sleep. Not a soul stirred in the hotel. It was certainly very early—perhaps too early to order breakfast? As if in reply to my question, I heard a clock in an adjacent room strike five. What should I do on such a lovely morning? Wake the others? I felt that this gesture might not be well received, especially by my wife! As I was quite sure that I could not go to sleep again, I made up my mind to go for a walk on my own.

Puente del Inca is the last inhabited locality on the road to Aconcagua and stands at an altitude of 8,850 feet. It gets its name from a natural bridge of rock, whose graceful arch, 150 feet in length, spans the muddy waters of the River of Las Cuevas, 130 feet below, and the width of this remarkable work of nature has permitted the construction of a motor road. The general effect is very colourful, for neighbouring hot springs have deposited a limestone covering of a brilliant yellow. These springs, which will petrify anything in the course of three weeks, are renowned throughout Argentina for their therapeutic properties. They cure rheumatism and nervous ailments, and if one is to believe a local legend, one of them—the "Spring of Love"—has even more wonderful attributes.

I took a track leading into the hills. The hamlet of Puente del Inca lay below me, with its hotel occupying the most important place. It was built in 1910 by the

48

British shareholders of the railway, and now belongs to the "Fondation Eva Peron". Close by is a small chapel, and on the other side of the river the Transandean railway station. The rest of the village consists of the post office, police station, military barracks and some other buildings housing hotel and office staffs.

The wonderful situation and the close proximity of Aconcagua attract a daily flood of tourists, but owing to the lack of modern comforts, few stay for very long. Considerable improvements are, however, *en train*, and a new hotel, more modern thermal baths, and a ski-lift will do much to make it a sought-after resort.

Time was getting on, so I turned back and made my way down to the hotel and breakfast.

An hour later we were all assembled with our baggage in the Army garage. Atilio now told me that our boxes were much too large and, above all, too heavy to be loaded on to the pack-mules. Each mule is supposed to carry 180 lb., which, when the weight of harness is deducted, leaves a useful load of 140 lb. There was only one thing to do—open the boxes and redistribute the food and equipment. For this very purpose we had some excellent leather bags, each holding 70 lb., and specially designed for pack-animals.

At first sight it all seemed extremely easy, but when we realised that we had to deal with two tons of baggage, it was quite another matter. "Good! . . . Well, what are we waiting for? . . . Let's get on with it."

Armed with a hammer and chisel, I gave the signal for attack. Within the space of a few minutes, equipped with every available engineering tool, the entire party gave itself wholeheartedly to this task. The primeval instinct of destruction was awakened, and disembodied boxes revealed their hidden treasures to the accompaniments of wild cries and breaking wood.

The soldiers looked on aghast, for the scene must have resembled the plunder of a ship by pirates rather than the preparations for departure of inoffensive mountaineers. In no time at all there was nothing left to break up.

Atilio rigged up a weighing machine and we started filling the first leather bag. So as not to exceed the agreed weight, we began to get together a varied assortment of essential articles, such as tinned foods, ropes, tents, air mattresses, pitons, crampons and the like, taking special care that they should not damage each other during the journey. Everybody voiced his own opinion; and in twenty minutes, after many false starts, the first bag was ready. We were inordinately proud of this fine achievement until Lucien, always the sarcastic one, bitingly remarked: "Well, chaps, at this rate you'll have finished the job in exactly eighteen hours and forty minutes from now."

Somewhat piqued, Guy retorted that there was no hurry, as our mules had not yet arrived from Uspallata. "That's quite true," I said. "We've got plenty of time. If all goes well, the mules will get here tomorrow—Thursday—after having done the fifty miles from Uspallata to Puente del Inca in one go. They will naturally be very tired, so we couldn't use them before Saturday morning at the earliest."

"Therefore," said Guy, "if we take an hour over each bag, we shall be ready in time."

In actual fact neither he nor anyone else wanted to get on with the tedious job, which fortunately was interrupted by the lunch bell.

Considering that we had done enough work for one day, I gave everybody the afternoon off, which we all spent in lounging about. Some read, others played canasta, while a few went for a walk and admired the mountains.

The morning of January 20th found us once more in the garage at work on the bags. We went hard at it, determined to finish this thankless task which kept us from enjoying our last few days of leisure. A suggestion made by Atilio to go on mules up to Lake Horcones galvanised us into renewed activity.

Busy as bees, we rushed about from bag to bag in the midst of an uproar which failed to conceal a certain amount of confusion in our actions.

"Pass the heavy stuff" (this was pitons, karabiner and tinned foods).

"Hoy! Chuck over a mattress and some spaghetti; I've loads of room."

"If you want to fill a bag with spaghetti," said a voice, "lie down in it."

Always a sense of humour!

The loads already finished, and firmly tied on to poles, extended the full length of the garage. Just before lunch the last load was completed and put with the others. There were so many that it needed more than thirty mules to carry them.

Lunch, like all other meals at this hotel, was excellent and almost too plentiful. We ate like giants in order to build up our strength for the hard work ahead of us; but a great disadvantage of these gargantuan repasts, washed down with first-class wine, was that we were seized with an irresistible desire to sleep. Today, however, as work was over, we surrendered to our longing for the siesta.

About 5 p.m. we were back in the courtyard, where soldiers were waiting with our mules. As I alone knew anything about mules, I was certainly the only one of the party who looked forward to the performance with any equanimity. It was more than evident that there was an air of apprehension about the others, and this was confirmed by one glance at Adrien. He was looking quizzically at the mules and at the same time fingering his wrist, doubtless trying to find the line of the fracture which was the outcome of his last escapade on horseback.

"*Vamos . . . mulas.*" These cries, accompanied by whistles and oaths, started the little caravan on its way.

All went well—so well, in fact, that at the end of ten minutes everyone was looking at everyone else with legitimate pride. Adrien in particular, anxious to demolish a well-established legend, was prancing about with an air of abandon. Only Suzanne seemed to be in difficulties. Her mule knew quite well that it was carrying a good friend who would not ill treat it for the world. It was quietly bringing up the rear when one of the soldiers gave it a great belt with his whip, which quickly recalled it to a sense of its responsibility.

As soon as we entered the Valley of Horcones I made a careful examination of the South Face through my field-glasses. But it was very difficult to pick out details, owing to the glare from the glaciers. Rather than be dazzled any longer, I preferred to enjoy the awe-inspiring spectacle.

There, bathed in sunlight, was the white crest of Aconcagua, framed between huge walls, far above the grumbling torrent in the gorges, its enormous precipices of rock and scree reaching to the sky.

Adrien, with his passion for photography, was in full blast. He was so busy with his films and various devices that we found it difficult to persuade him that the time had come to return to the hotel.

There was no news of the mules coming from Uspallata. This was very annoying, for it held up our departure, and I was anxious to be off. The weather had been fine for a week, but every day I feared a change; besides which, I was in a hurry—a very great hurry—to come to grips with the problem.

Two days went by and the barometer remained steady at "Fine". Still no mules, so we continued to kill time with canasta and walks. Ultimately they arrived, and that evening we partook of our last dinner at Puente del Inca. We had champagne, and as the corks popped I could not refrain from thinking how much more they would do so when we returned victorious, for we had made up our minds to fight to the bitter end.

ALMACEN (THE SHOP)

THE GIGANTIC PRECIPICES OF THE SOUTH ARÈTE OF ACONCAGUA

Sunday January 24th

A long caravan, fifty-seven mules in all, stretched out down the track crossing the last pasturages of Puente del Inca. In the cold morning air Aconcagua looked even higher and more distant than ever, almost ethereal with its snow-plume blown by the wind. The silence of the dawn was broken only by the cries of the soldiers, each of whom was "towing" two pack-animals behind his mule, accompanied by much shouting and swearing.

Mario Pasten, the *baquiano* of Aconcagua, led the caravan. A *baquiano* is not quite the same as a guide, as understood in Europe. Owing to the absence of peasantry in the Cordilleras, there are no local guides, and one is forced to utilise the services of "a man who knows intimately a certain section of the mountains"—in other words, the *baquiano*. Normally he does not go higher than a mule will take him, but up to that time he has complete charge of the party and is responsible for getting the loads to base camp, or even higher.

Our man, on the contrary, had twice ascended Aconcagua, and I am sure that he knew the mountain better than anyone for a hundred miles round.

Leaving Atilio and Pasten to continue on their way, I stopped for a few minutes by Lake Horcones. At this early hour there was not a breath of wind and the limpid waters were as calm as a mirror, wherein was reflected the image of Aconcagua. But I had no time for dreams, and tearing myself away from this entrancing spectacle, I spurred on my mule and overtook the party.

The green grass along the edge of the lake gave place to drab vegetation, as dry and hardy as its perverseness in growing amidst the stones. We crossed the River Horcones opposite to where it was joined by the stream of El Duragno. Fortunately the water was low, so that at even the deepest part of the ford it did not reach higher than the mules' bellies. Apart from the soldiers,

E 53

hampered by the pack-animals, we got across this potentially dangerous river without any incidents.

The valley had now narrowed to a deep gorge, and the path began to mount a steep scree slope; further on it disappeared altogether among large blocks or crumbling moraine. It could nowhere be compared with some of the worst paths found in the Alps—in fact the mules scarcely noticed it, and, plodding along at a regular pace, brought us to Confluencia by about 10 a.m.

As its name suggests, Confluencia is the junction of the two Horcones Valleys: the Upper, descending from the north slopes of Aconcagua, and the Lower, which has its source on the south side.

We were about to leave the classic route of Plaza de Mulas, site of base camps on the normal way up the mountain; but before doing so it was necessary to pause and reassemble the caravan, which was straggling along several miles in the rear.

The peaks of Tolosa, Dedos and Mexico, all exceeding 5,000 m. (16,400 feet) in height, limited our vision to the left. These high mountains were nothing but vast ruins, consisting of disintegrating rock, tottering towers overhanging immense red-and-grey scree slopes. There was an indescribable air of desolation about this burnt-up area.

Pasten started up the high scree slopes; the track had vanished, and his mule sank up to the hocks in the loose stones. However, the animal performed extraordinary evolutions in an altogether surprising manner on this shifting surface. Our confidence restored, we followed in its tracks, finally reaching the end of the valley close to the snout of the Lower Horcones Glacier. In its crevassed, tormented state, covered with stones resembling scales, this glacier might have been a monster escaped from the Apocalypse. 16,700 feet above us to the right soared the peak of Almacen, displaying its multi-coloured strata. (Almacen means "shop", derived from the hori-

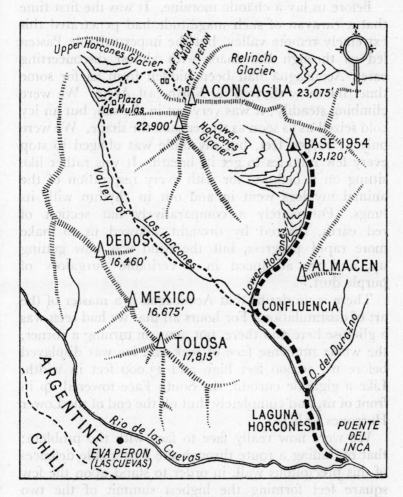

THE ACONCAGUA MASSIF, WITH ITS PRINCIPAL SUMMITS, SHOWING THE
APPROACH ROUTE

zontal and regular arrangement of its strata, resembling shelves.)

Before us lay a chaotic moraine. It was the first time that a caravan of such magnitude had penetrated this extremely remote valley, but the imperturbable Pasten led us through the chaos with almost disconcerting ease. Aconcagua had been hidden from us for some time, but now showed its North-east Arête. We were climbing steadily; it was very hot in the sun, but an icy cold seized us as soon as we reached the shade. We were only at 12,450 feet, but my mule was obliged to stop every few minutes to get its breath. It was rather like sitting on a bellows, for with every respiration of the animal my legs went in and out in rhythm with its lungs. Fortunately a comparatively flat section of red earth, fissured by drought, allowed us to make more rapid progress, but the wind was now getting up, and we advanced in a veritable purgatory of purple dust.

There is no doubt that Aconcagua is a master of the art of dissimulation. For hours all that we had seen was a glimpse here and there, but now, on turning a corner, the whole immense face of rock and ice was displayed before us, 10,000 feet high and 23,000 feet in width. Like a gigantic curtain, the South Face towered up in front of us, and completely shut off the end of the Lower Horcones Valley.

We were now really face to face with the problem: that of finding a route through the formidable defences of this precipitous wall, in order to stand upon the few square feet forming the highest summit of the two American continents. What did it matter whether the peak was a few feet higher or lower than the 7,000 m. (22,960 feet) attributed to it by the surveyors? All such banal calculations lose their value when one stands before the majesty of this stupendous face.

We went on slowly side by side, and all our comments

on the spectacle were aptly summed up by Robert's remark: "Well, boys, it looks ruddy awful!"

The first and most important thing to do was to find a suitable site for our Base Camp. Several factors entered into this. In the first place, it must be as close to the face as possible, in order to obviate the necessity of carrying heavy loads for long distances; in the second, it must be protected from stones falling from the ridge joining Almacen to the North Arête of Aconcagua. There must also be a convenient water supply, and the ground must be hard enough for a camp to be built on it. The ideal site would, of course, combine all these factors in a place sheltered from the wind.

Quite close to the glacier we found a fine level expanse sheltered from the wind on three sides, but unfortunately it was a long way from the Face and covered with a thick layer of dust. As I had no wish to make it easier for the wind to mix the dust with our food—which it would probably do anyhow—I went on ahead with Atilio to explore.

I saw what looked like a suitable spot at the foot of a small rock spur and decided to make a closer inspection. It turned out to be a little terrace of hard earth, protected from stone-fall by the rock spur, with a small stream close by. It was about 150 feet above the glacier and had a fine view over the valley. The only drawback was that it was very exposed to the wind. However, we were not likely to find anything better, so I chose it.

It was 2 p.m. when we began to unload the mules. The sight of food being unpacked reminded Edmond that he had not eaten.

"Well, what about it? I'm absolutely starving!"

"Yes, that's right," added Pierre; "we haven't had anything the whole way."

Everyone immediately began to feel immensely hungry. Atilio had thought of everything—cold meat, cheese and even wine appeared as if by magic. We ate in silence, our eyes on the Face. We had now ceased to be so hungry, possibly owing to the height, or it may have been due to the sticky dust on the food.

The soldiers were finishing unloading the mules and had piled all our goods and chattels in the middle of the terrace, which we christened "Plaza Nueva Argentina". As soon as the last load was on the ground, Atilio re-assembled his caravan and went back to Puente del Inca, leaving two volunteers with us. He was to return with more loads in two days' time.

Left alone and confronted with the heap of equipment and food, already covered with dust, we realised that the expedition was now really about to start. I sat down on a stone and, thinking of all the effort it had cost us to get this far, remarked that we had completed the first lap—and now for the second!

Pierre shook us out of our lethargy.

"Come on, chaps, get cracking; we've got to get the tents up."

The wind bellied out the canvas like a thing possessed, and it took four men to hold it down. While they were struggling with it, the rest of us gathered large stones to act as anchors. In order to reduce wind resistance, we buried the tent a little in the ground. As soon as we had got it up, we tied it down with ropes and heaped earth and stones on the sides.

It was indeed a pleasure to be in a tent full of memories —it took our minds off this bleak spot.

Originally brought to France by the U.S. Army, it had been used every summer at Chamonix by climbers from the Club Olympique de Billancourt.

"Who knows? Perhaps it was the one I used," said Robert.

"Yours or not, we've got to put up another one for the food."

"What are we going to do with that one over there?"

"It's the largest; it'll do for the mess-tent."

"That's all very well," said Edmond; "but where are we going to sleep? We should be all right in that one."

"Like everyone else, you'll sleep in the little tent," retorted Adrien; "and, what's more, I've found just the place for them—about thirty yards from here."

As soon as we had pitched the store-tent, next door to the mess-tent, our two soldiers started putting in the provisions. We then went off to look at the suggested site for our sleeping quarters, which, if not perhaps quite as suitable as we expected, was at least sheltered from the wind.

One by one—bright spots in the wilderness—our tents were pitched in this sombre desert of rock and stone. Suddenly a tremendous roar broke the silence. A colossal avalanche swept down the central couloir, just on the other side of our rock spur. Holding our breath, we watched the huge snow-cloud cross the mile-wide glacier and mount the other side of the valley. Then came a second one, smaller in extent, at the same spot. It had barely reached the glacier when yet a third avalanche rumbled down, a little further to the right. What a reception!

The atmosphere here in our tent was heavy. Everyone squatted in his corner, much more preoccupied with thoughts of the Face than with the meal. The lack of light also added to the general air of depression, for the lamps and batteries had been inadvertently left behind at Puente del Inca. We were reduced for this evening to using an incredible lamp manufactured from a food-tin and a shoe-lace dipped in olive oil, which spread a subdued and rather sooty radiance over the proceedings.

Outside in the bitter air scintillated the luminous firmament so common to night at high altitude. The wind had completely died away and the silence was absolute. Like ghosts, the glaciers on the Face glimmered in the darkness.

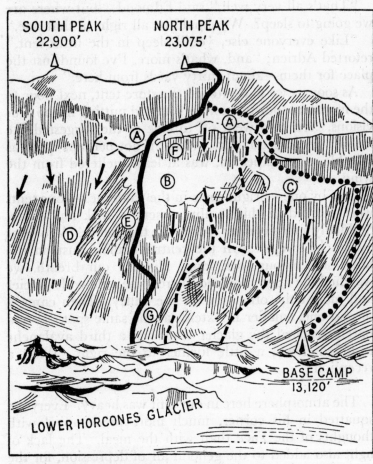

SOUTH PEAK
22,900'

NORTH PEAK
23,075'

A

F

B

E

D

G

A

C

BASE CAMP
13,120'

LOWER HORCONES GLACIER

●●●● Route suggested by Saint-Loup
– – – "S" Route (suggested)
▬▬ Route up the Central Spur as carried out
↓ Direction of avalanches

THE VARIOUS ROUTES SUGGESTED FOR THE ASCENT OF THE SOUTH FACE

A. Upper Glacier   D. Great Couloir
B. Middle Glacier   E. Central Spur
C. Grey Glacier   F. Rock Wall
G. Bergschrund at foot of Face

Just as on the first night at Puente del Inca, I was thinking too much of the Face to be able to sleep, and tossed and turned from side to side in my sleeping-bag. Judging from the sounds of creaking mattresses coming from the other tents, I gathered that I was not the only one suffering from insomnia. Suzanne had taken a sleeping pill, but without any apparent success.

Even the mules seemed restless, for I could hear their chains rattling. They made such a noise that it was almost as if they were trying to escape. I did not like this, for when animals are restless I always wonder whether it may be due to an instinct warning them against some unknown danger.

Was it premonition or just coincidence? At this moment a terrific cannonade broke out and large rocks began to fall somewhere high up on the spur above us. Suzanne, terrified, started up with a stifled cry. I jumped up and looked out of the tent and saw rocks bounding down to the glacier below. The night frost was expanding the water under the loose stones, and soon a second avalanche roared down. With a noise of thunder, huge rocks swept down the left side of the spur, striking showers of sparks in their passage. They went the same way as the others, and thus assured me of the safety of our site.

The tent was now full of acrid fumes from the pulverised flint, and Suzanne, whose nerves were on edge, started to cry. Everyone began to ask questions, so I made a hasty tour of the camp and reassured them all. Outside, the pale crests, caressed by the moon, resumed their eternal silence.

Monday January 25th

It was a glorious day, like all the others since we had reached the mountains. A light breeze was blowing from the valley. The rock-fall of the night before had swept down the bed of our stream, leaving a thin stream of

61

dirty water flowing among the stones. Our breakfast tasted of dust.

The two soldiers looked after the kitchen, placed in the shelter of a large rock, while the rest of us searched the Face with our field-glasses. In spite of its size we gradually familiarised ourselves with it, in so far as we coined nicknames for certain outstanding features and obvious cracks in its armour.

In direct line below the main summit there was a very steep rock wall some hundreds of feet high supporting two glaciers, which were situated symmetrically to the east and west of the peak and edged by séracs. Right in the centre of the Face, at about 19,700 feet, the "Upper Glacier" was in places between 350 and 650 feet thick, but it was not very steep and led us to think that, once reached, the worst difficulties would be over. Below the "Rock Wall" which sustained the Upper Glacier was a hanging glacier. It was very crevassed, and, owing to its position in the centre of the Face, we christened it the "Middle Glacier". A rock buttress on its right separated it from the "Grey Glacier". This was partially covered with stones and nieves penitentes (ice-needles caused by ablation) and was almost level. Huge curtains of ice hung down from its séracs.

These hanging glaciers, festooned with threatening séracs, provided the real problem of the ascent of the South Face—how to avoid ice avalanches.

Apart from the Central Couloir, which was obviously too dangerous, there were two possibilities open to us, in addition to the route suggested by Saint Loup, which we did not propose to attempt. It was certainly safe from avalanches; but the bottom half was not a direct ascent of the Face, and we did not wish to deviate from this in any way.

This left two routes for consideration. The first was the S route, so called by reason of its many bends. It went right up the Face, but all the lower part was subjected to constant avalanches from the Middle Glacier. From a technical standpoint it was relatively easy, and as up to the present the avalanches had been confined to the Central Couloir, it attracted certain members of the party. Those against it, however, based their opinion on the fact that, even so, the avalanche danger was too great on the lower part, added to which there did not appear to be any safe camp-sites. This left the Central Spur.

As this route was in direct line to the summit, it was the most attractive of all. The crest of the buttress, well protected from avalanches, ascended in a straight line to the base of the Upper Glacier. A detailed examination of the route revealed, however, several vital "technical problems". The first of these was a series of vertical towers just below the Middle Glacier. They were more than 260 feet in height, and cut by chimneys, probably full of ice. Higher up, a pronounced overhang split by cracks marked the centre of the Rock Wall. Finally there were the séracs of the Upper Glacier. In view of what we had observed during our flight across the Face, we were confident of being able to cope with them; so, after a fresh discussion, the majority of us, strongly backed by myself, decided to attempt the Central Spur.

In the meantime the morning breeze had freshened to a gale, and, coming down from the South Col of Aconcagua, raised clouds of dust. The flags were flapping violently against their poles in the centre of the camp.

We returned to camp, as we feared for the safety of the tents. The canvas, furiously assailed by the squalls, seemed likely to pull out the guy-ropes—in fact some of them were already loose. We rapidly strengthened the anchorage, when suddenly, without warning, a gust of unusual violence crossed the camp, broke my tent-pole and carried away Guy's and Lucien's tent. Half suffocated and blinded, our mouths and nostrils full of dust, we watched the catastrophe develop. Three hundred feet above our heads, the tent spilled its contents over the countryside.

Air mattresses, sleeping-bags, shirts and other garments floated about in the air; a few moments later they landed far away on a scree slope.

When calm was restored we set off in pursuit of our belongings. Fearing that another blast might carry them even further away, we tried to run, but the height proved too much and we had to stop. Puffing like grampuses, it took us more than an hour to collect everything. The total damage amounted to three tents unserviceable, two shirts and two sleeping-bags torn and two mattresses punctured.

"There is no doubt," said Robert, "that the Face is putting up a good resistance!"

Before eating, we struck the remaining tents and, to make assurance doubly sure, weighted them down with large stones.

When night fell we used the mess-tent as sleeping quarters. The wind was still blowing great guns, and dust penetrated everywhere. Avalanches continued to rumble down the face.

Tuesday January 26th

We got up at 9 a.m. The wind had continued all night; we felt dirty and tired. The first avalanches were coming down the S route, and in order to tease Adrien, who favoured that ascent, Lucien said "Well, Didi, what about making a recce up the S?"

He made no reply, but asked Pierre to accompany him to the foot of the Face to study the assault on the Central Spur!

A few minutes later they both disappeared along the moraine. An hour went by, and with our field-glasses we could see them walking about close to the bergschrund.

"Here's the caravan; there are at least thirty mules."

We turned and searched the bottom of the valley. There it was crossing the wide tract of red earth which we had named "Arizona".

Just at that moment a loud roar directed our attention to the Face. Two avalanches, both from the Upper Glacier, were pouring down close to the Spur; they were unusually large. Hiding part of the wall, the two clouds of snow united, reached the glacier at the foot and spread out. With some anxiety I searched for my two comrades with my glasses; they must be somewhere in the danger zone. At last I found them sitting on a rock watching the spectacle, fortunately well out of range. It was a bit of luck that their stall seats were not too far in front!

The caravan arrived, but Atilio had not come up. At last we had got everything with us. Edmond, who was fed up with oil lamps, was looking through our cases for the electric lamps, when, lifting a lid, he gave a whistle of surprise: "Jolly good; there's some booze!"

We appreciated this gesture all the more since we had been suffering from colic for two days as a result of drinking the water from the stream. The mules had also brought some building material for the hut and a large tent, which we erected at once.

In the meantime Adrien and Pierre had come back, very pleased with their reconnaissance. They said that the avalanches did not touch the Spur, which was affected only by the clouds of snow. Pierre concluded, "It's going to be a hard job, but we'll do it all right."

These encouraging remarks, together with a few glasses of wine, caused a rapid rise in our morale. To-morrow we would attack. . . .

The caravan went down again, still leaving us two soldiers, one a replacement, for the other absolutely refused to stay any longer in this desolate spot. The new man, Mercedes Oroda, seemed a nice fellow, and I felt we should soon be friends.

After a pleasant lunch, we re-arranged the store-tent.

The air was dry and the wind was still with us, blowing the inevitable dust everywhere. I put our ice-axes in the stream in order to swell the hafts, which were completely dried up.

Edmond and Lucien tried their hand at cooking, and turned out a roast which we literally lapped up. We took a long time over the meal, and it wasn't until quite late that the cold drove us into our sleeping-bags. Behind Almacen, lightning was stabbing the darkness, and a storm was raging over Mendoza. If only the weather would hold!

The tents seemed full of static electricity: sleeping sacks, nylon vests and one's hair produced long sparks on the slightest friction. The wind was still blowing, causing the canvas to flap and the tent-poles to creak dismally. Batuque, Mercedes' dog, howled all through the night.

Wednesday January 27th

We rose early, in spite of a dreadful night. Wind, dust, avalanches, falling stones—all the elements seemed in league for the purpose of sapping our morale. The weather had not changed, but, unfortunately, neither had the wind. One party set off to reconnoitre the spur, its object being to cross the bergschrund, place fixed ropes if necessary and find a site for Camp I.

Another party started in the direction of a nameless col on the arête above us. It had no special mission, except that of acclimatisation and of satisfying our natural curiosity as to what lay on the other side.

The spur party returned to Base Camp at about 3 p.m. It had fixed 100 feet of rope over the schrund, making it quite easy to cross. Above it, steep slopes of broken rock, somewhat exposed to stone-fall, led to a possible site for one tent. After a good deal of levelling and building up it might be possible to erect another. Still higher up, broken rock, quite easy but dangerous, continued to the crest of the arête, which Lucien reached at about 13,100 feet. Further progress would appear to be difficult but practicable. It would take about three hours from Base Camp to Camp I, perhaps less when we were in training.

An hour later the second party got back. After three hours of hard work they had reached the col, which they called Col du Névé, via a dangerous scree-slope— "quite unmentionable", said Guy. This col, which derived its new name from a patch of snow on either side, was of no interest. Behind the arête there was a huge expanse of grey sand.

Everyone was now complaining of lack of breath— hardly surprising, for we had only been four days at 13,000 feet, and were neither sufficiently acclimatised nor in training.

About 6 p.m. large black clouds from the Pacific swept over the crests. Did they mean a change in the weather? Anything might be expected, with this eternal wind.

There was a universal request for another roast. In order to celebrate our first encounter with the Face, we organised a real banquet. After coffee, Robert produced a bottle containing a colourless liquid made at Bullion (his birthplace). We quaffed the fiery draught, and Lucien said, *sotto voce*, "If we run out of fuel, we can always burn Robert's fire-water."

This was a gratuitous insult, which Robert (and everyone else) literally swallowed! Soon pipes and cigarettes were going and Guy launched forth on the evergreen and inexhaustible subject of mountain stories. Memories of Fontainebleau, Chamonix or Aconcagua, they were all the same; we knew them by heart, but liked them all none the less for that.

Through the open door we could see the Face, or rather the part that was free of cloud. We did not go to bed until very late—or was it very early? There was not a star to be seen and it was very mild. It looked very like a break-up of the weather.

Thursday January 28th

"Is this blasted wind never going to stop?" grumbled Lucien. As he was near the door, he was in an admirable position for "collecting all the dust going", as he said. Every morning it was the same: he awoke in a furious state of mind to find his sleeping-bag and clothes covered with "this filthy mess".

The strong gusts caused the tent-poles to bend in an ominous manner. The ridge-pole was creaking and threatening to break. If that happened, it would be a real disaster, for the canvas would tear and we would have to add another tent to the pile of those already useless, which we had put under a rock out of the way.

A guy-rope broke with a crack like a whip and the tent shook in a most disturbing manner. We rushed out to put it right, dressed only in shirts, stung by the biting wind and covered with dust.

Ugly-looking clouds were streaming across the Face. They broke up crossing the arête, but re-formed on the Upper Glacier. Fierce winds emanating from the South Col swept across the glacier. It looked bad, and we should have to make a decision very soon.

The first requisite of a good base camp is that it should provide the maximum of comfort and rest. We were quite aware of this, but at the same time realised that unless we got complete shelter from the wind we should never achieve this laudable goal. We must at all costs evacuate this plateau where the winds never ceased. We might be able to find a more suitable site closer to the Face, perhaps on the scree slope descending to the stream. This, however, was likely to mean a great deal of levelling and building up before we had dug out a suitable site on the slope. We made our decision, and as soon as lunch was over started work.

It is not a particularly pleasant job to try to build a terrace at 13,000 feet; but we consoled ourselves with the

THE SOUTH FACE SEEN FROM BASE CAMP 13,120′ AT THE END OF THE LOWER
HORCONES GLACIER

THE SOUTH FACE FROM BASE CAMP

thought that we were getting acclimatised. We worked all day, stopping for a breather after every few blows with the axe. Soon we were covered with dust from head to foot, and, to make things worse, when the dust was mixed with perspiration it completely clogged our beards, until we looked like nothing on earth.

It took us another day before we had cut a platform big enough to hold three large tents.

We made quite certain this time, by tying them all together with climbing ropes attached to large stones, and then piling earth up high around them so that they made a homogeneous unit. This arrangement undoubtedly offered great resistance to the wind, but it presented some disadvantages as regards the snoring of certain members of the party! In order to get over this, we arranged to sleep in tents separated by the mess-tent. Our two soldiers, Mercedes and Antonio, slept in the store-tent, a few feet to the left and below us on another platform.

Saturday January 30th

During the night one of the mules broke loose and ran away. We were not much disturbed by this, as we were quite certain it knew its way back to Puente del Inca.

In spite of our prediction, the weather remained fine. The wind still swept across the plateau, but hardly affected our new camp site, which we found much better in every way than its predecessor.

While we were putting the finishing touches to the new camp, Edmond tried his skill as a barber on Robert, Pierre and Lucien. We had now been here six days, and although not yet quite in training, our acclimatisation was sufficiently advanced to permit us to think of establishing Camp I at the base of the spur. Having got everything ready, Mercedes set off with a mule to carry it all as close to the Face as possible. Next morning at about 8 a.m. we left Base Camp.

We wound our way briskly through the chaos of the moraine, erecting cairns as we went to mark the route. We caught up with the mules in a hollow close to a clear spring.

Bent almost double under the weight of the heavy sacks, with our noses up against the slope, we cursed the stones which slipped under our feet. Quite indifferent to the beauty of the scenery, we had eyes only for the feet of the man above us, and were fully occupied in stepping in his tracks. Having crossed the glacier, we started up the snow-slope leading to the bergschrund. We were obliged to hurry across a wide avalanche cone, which taxed our hearts and lungs to the utmost. Once across the bergschrund we used the fixed rope to scale a steep couloir full of debris. In spite of all our precautions, the stones poured down, causing considerable dismay to those members of the party who were awaiting their turn 100 feet below. Higher up we ascended over broken rock, bordering a couloir which canalised everything falling from the Middle Glacier. Although the terrain was occasionally dangerous owing to its steepness, it was not difficult enough to warrant the use of the rope, which in any case would have acted as a brake, and might have been a hindrance in the event of a stone-fall. But nothing happened, apart from the fall of a few isolated rocks which bounded down the couloir out of reach. After two hours of hard work we threw ourselves down exhausted on the site of our future Camp I.

This was a good position, as it was some distance from the couloir and protected by a bulge in the wall above. The ground was a trifle rough, but as we were by now expert platform-makers we were not unduly troubled.

We soon set to work with our ice-axes, and while some of us built a little retaining wall, the others filled up holes with earth and stones. A loud detonation followed by dull rumblings caused us to throw ourselves flat on the ground with our arms over our heads.

"There, in the couloir." A huge avalanche was coming down, and the stream of snow, ice and rocks swept past about two rope lengths away. A cloud of fine snow covered us, and when it had passed we could see the last blocks of ice rolling down the cone which we had crossed earlier. As Pierre remarked, it was definitely not a place in which to dally.

The platform was beginning to take shape. On one side a large rock refused to budge, in spite of the united efforts of Guy and myself. With the help of one of the others we finally got it to move. During my exertions I cracked my lumbar vertebrae. It was used to this, however, as it was not the first time it had happened. I straightened up and went on with my digging.

An hour later we had a fine platform, on which we erected a tent in which Guy and Lucien were to spend the night.

With our backs to the little wall, we remained for a good half-hour looking out over the valley, at the bottom of which we could see some tiny white shapes: the tents of the Base Camp. It was now time to go down.

"Well, it's not the whole story, but at last here we are! So long."

PART TWO : THE ASSAULT

by Guy Poulet

Chapter One

FIRST ENCOUNTER WITH THE FACE

AFTER a last hand-clasp our four friends disappeared in the direction of the slabs of the
couloir. Their departure imparted a sudden sense
of emptiness to the tiny terrace, so recently echoing to the sound of rolling stones, the grating of ice-axes
and friendly imprecations. We suddenly felt very much
alone, and for a moment we looked at each other a little
disconsolately, with a vague feeling of being faced with a
hostility harder to bear now that there were only three
of us.

For now Robert, Lucien and I were going to spend a
night on the mountain—admittedly only at its foot, but
nevertheless actually upon it for the first time in our little
high-altitude tent.

Robert was the first to break the silence:

"Well, come on, get cracking; we must fix the guy-
ropes and place stones to hold down the tent; and then
there's food to think of."

These words aroused us from our lethargy, and we got
busy moving some rocks to hold the tent down. Soon
everything was ready, and I went inside with Lucien
to adjust the silk lining. He gave a whistle of admiration:
"Good Lord, silk! We do ourselves pretty well."
Robert's head looked in from the other side: "Terrific,
we certainly are big-shots!"

We inflated our mattresses and then had to work out
the problem of sleeping, for we had only a two-man tent
for three persons. We finally decided that two would
sleep one way, while the third would sleep head to feet

in between, the third mattress, half inflated, serving as his pillow. Now for the kitchen. This consisted quite simply of a compressed-gas cooker balanced on a more or less flat rock. Robert took exception to this stone, to which I replied that I couldn't be bothered to find a better one, and anyhow it was flat enough for the purpose.

"That's all very fine, but supposing the cooker rolls down to the glacier; it won't be so funny."

At this moment Lucien arrived carrying two tins full of water and, taking in the situation at a glance, solved the problem.

"It's quite easy; you've only got to put a sack in front, and if the cooker topples over, it will be stopped by the sack."

Robert shook his head without conviction and went off muttering to himself about upset tins and spoiled soup.

At this moment we saw four dots far below on the glacier, winding in and out between crevasses and the first rocks of the moraine. We looked at our watches—they had taken only half an hour to get down.

We went to the edge of the terrace and shouted. They stopped for an instant, and from their attitude we could guess that they were looking in our direction, then they went on and disappeared behind a projection of the moraine.

It was still quite light, but we were in the shade; the sun had disappeared behind the South Col, while below, the glacier lay bathed in sunshine. When we looked up at the Face, we could see the band of séracs shining in the sun; much higher, the two summits stood out against the intense blue of the sky. They seemed very far away and almost overhanging. Nearer at hand the ice-fall of the Middle Glacier was also in the shade, while the end of the Spur appeared to lose itself in thin air, looking like an absurd heap of stones which led nowhere.

We began to feel cold, and put on our anoraks. Everyone had his own special hat, chosen according to his own taste, as we had not evolved a standard type of headgear for the expedition as a whole. The water in the tins was beginning to sing as we watched Robert's efforts at concocting mushroom soup—our first real high-altitude meal. The shadows of the mountain were lengthening on the glacier, for all the world like the jaws of a trap closing very slowly.

"They won't have the sun at Base Camp much longer," remarked Lucien.

We turned and looked down on the glacier. Seen from here, the tents appeared closer together, as if they were trying to get warm by their close proximity to each other. Our friends must have got there by now. A fall of stones somewhere above us made us turn round and listen attentively.

"Down there, to the right, below the séracs."

The stones bounded down the couloir, bringing blocks of ice with them. The hiss of the soup boiling over attracted our attention.

"It's ready," said Lucien.

"You really think so?"

"Of course; as soon as it boiled over."

"Let's leave it a bit; it takes longer to boil higher up."

It was finally agreed that the soup was indeed ready, and we set to, burning ourselves in the process, dipping our spoons in the same tin. In the meanwhile we had put a tin of sausages to warm up on the cooker, but by the time they were ready we had lost our appetite, and anyhow they did not look very nice. We now decided to make a hot grog, but found we had left the wine down below, so had to make do with Ovomaltine, which cheered us enormously.

We lit cigarettes and searched for a comfortable spot to await the light-signals from Base Camp. It was nine o'clock, and we were to expect them at 9.30 p.m. The sky was still quite clear, and the séracs at the top of the mountain were bathed in sunshine. We were all doubtless thinking of when we should be up there ourselves, above the séracs, where the sun still shines at nine o'clock in the evening.

But just now we had a more pressing thought which had obsessed each and every one of us ever since we arrived here. It had been chewed over in our minds, and now it began to come out, at first casually, in our conversation.

"This incessant stone-fall gets on your nerves."

"Yes, you can't get used to it; it makes me jump every time."

"You never know whether it's coming down on your head."

"And these avalanches; they're not little ones, either; there are great rocks in them and . . ."

"I know; nevertheless, I think that our platform is safe."

This, indeed, was the crux of the problem—were we really safe from falling stones or avalanches? There had been no choice of site; could we sleep peacefully in our tent?

This mood soon gave place to a spell of comforting activity. We carefully scrutinised the fall-line of the Spur, the adjacent couloirs and the two bands of séracs which dominated it. We even crawled about on hands and knees looking for signs of recent impact on the terrace. But the only one we found had come from a rock which we had dislodged ourselves while constructing the platform for the tent.

After a fresh examination, during the course of which we drew upon our knowledge of all sorts of complex sciences, such as ballistics, geology and relativity, we arrived at a favourable conclusion, and as it was 9.25 p.m, we rushed for our torches. Seated facing the valley, with our backs to the wall, we awaited the first signals from below, while trying to work out a method of synchronisation for our three lamps. The code was simple enough: all's well—three clear separate signals, repeated three times; if all was not well . . . we now realised that we had nothing worked out for that eventuality! We were ready now; when Lucien said "Click", we all switched on, when he said "Clack", we switched off—simple, but practical! We were playing around like kids who had just discovered a new game, when suddenly we saw the first signal from Base Camp. They must have got out the large hurricane lamp, which they alternately covered and uncovered with a cloth. We replied enthusiastically with our "clicks" and "clacks", but the code was rapidly exhausted, so we abandoned ourselves to a regular orgy of confused winkings and blinkings. The lamp at Base Camp also seemed to be similarly affected. All this went on for some time, and then the light disappeared: they had gone back into their tents.

Once more we were alone; the cold began to make itself felt; it was time to prepare for the night. We were now feeling the effect of our efforts during the day: our muscles were stiff, and despite two layers of warm clothing we were shivering. Moreover, we were all suffering from slight headaches, either as a result of fatigue or reaction to the height. After a last look at the summit, we turned in.

Now began a series of contortions and crawlings amid a confusion of anoraks, coats and boots. The interior of the tent was only about 2 feet 6 inches high, and if one wanted to take one's trousers off, it was necessary to perform subtle and quite reptilian gymnastic feats. This was further complicated when the victim tried to slide into his sleeping-bag, and at the moment there were only two of us—Lucien and myself—in the tent.

Robert was sitting at the entrance urging us to hurry and finish our nocturnal preparations. We, on our part, threw out a few thinly disguised hints as to how much better it would be for him to bivouac outside, in view of the fact that the tent was made to hold only two, and that, with his robust constitution . . . It was a wasted effort: Robert remained unconvinced and, cutting short our remarks, he came in as well, feet first. The tent bulged ominously, and for a few moments we just glared at one another. However, calm was gradually restored, and we sorted ourselves out with sighs of relief. This peace did not last long, for one of us suddenly said: "The sleeping pills!"

Consternation reigned. In order to be assured of a good night's slumber for the first night, at any rate, we had brought "hypnotic" tablets with us, and had completely forgotten them until we were settled in. I was supposed to be in charge of the medicine chest but despite wriggling and rummaging in my sack, I was unable to find them. I said in an airy manner to Robert that the box of tablets was in his sack, which was under his head, and that all he had to do was to turn over and find them. He replied in a furious tone that contrary to appearances, it was not his sack under his head, but Lucien's; he had put his under him to wedge the mattress.

The tent was once more turned upside down, and at last the pills came to light.

But it was not as easy as all that: we were so jammed together that taking the beastly tablets became a major operation involving a complete reorganisation of our ménage. At last we were able to relax—as much as it was possible to do so—stretch out on our mattresses and try to sleep.

I curled myself up in my bag, but sleep would not

come. Tensed up, I heard stones rattling down the couloirs: the waterfall down the Central Couloir had frozen up, but the mountain was anything but silent. One could sense its living presence by movement of the stones caused by the frost, the hanging glaciers relentlessly pushing forward their masses of ice towards the edge of the precipices above us. And all we had for protection against these latent threats were two thicknesses of nylon and silk!

I looked at my luminous watch, which gave out a friendly light in the darkness—half-past one already.

I tried reasoning with myself: "You clot! Go to sleep. You're perfectly safe—nothing can fall on you: you're protected by large overhangs. Yes, but supposing stones fall from the overhang itself. . . ."

I tried another tack—fatalism. "Right, there's nothing one can do about it. If we are going to be killed by an avalanche, so what! We can't alter it; so why not go to sleep? You'll need all your strength tomorrow for the climb. Relax. . . ."

I felt Lucien turning over next to me. I couldn't keep quiet any longer, and spoke to him in a low voice:

"Lucien, are you asleep?"

"Well, I'm trying to."

"These falling stones, do you think we're taking a great risk?"

"No; at the worst they will be fairly close, but they are not likely to touch us unless a whole mass of séracs comes down at once, and even then . . ."

All of a sudden there was the sound of sharp explosions, followed by an impact, then silence; rocks ricocheted, and then a noise which made my heart bound: the vibration of a rock falling through the air.

"Good God! this is it."

We all turned at the same time and thrust our heads outside the tent. Far away to the left a shower of sparks

81

rose from the slabs below the South Summit; it was 500 feet to our left.

We lay down again, and I could feel Robert's legs relaxing.

"Look, we shall have to let our nerves relax if we're going to get any sleep."

I turned over and faced the mountain. I could hear my heart beating, and I kept an ear open for noises coming from outside.

"You silly fool, keep calm; breathe deeply and count up to a hundred. You came up here of your own free will—nobody forced you to—and now you will go to sleep; it's vital."

This bit of auto-suggestion had the desired effect, and I fell into a sort of intermittent doze.

At 7.45 a.m. the first rays of the sun gilded our tent, and through the opening we could see a piece of blue sky.

All our fears of the past night vanished in a flash. We opened wide the tent door and, lying flat on our mattresses, regarded what we could see of the Face. The sky was pale blue and the light fell softly on our faces; it was going to be like a day in the holidays.

For a moment we enjoyed this pleasant feeling of well-being to the full, before we plunged into intense activity. First of all we had to crawl out of our warm sleeping-bags, get dressed and go outside one at a time. It was still cold, despite the sunshine. We took deep breaths and rubbed our hands vigorously. The cooker containing our breakfast—chocolate with condensed milk, biscuits and jam—was singing. Then we got ready our sacks.

We decided not to take too much, for we were not yet fully acclimatised. We intended to limit ourselves to climbing equipment other than ice-axes and crampons, which in any case would be quite useless on the rocky spur. We made a very careful selection of rock pitons, and took a fairly complete assortment, ranging from the large U-section type (broches) to the short, thin type (extra-plats). Robert hesitated for a moment and then added three angle pitons to his collection.

"These," he said, "are really super; they hold very well, and one can always knock them in."

Two rock hammers, twenty karabiner, two 170-foot nylon ropes and 80 feet of alpine line completed our loads, which we distributed among our three sacks, carefully checking each sack for weight. To drink we took a bottle of slightly sweetened cold tea, and with some bars of nougat and dried fruit in our pockets, we left Camp I at 9 a.m.

To begin with, we advanced together, unroped, for the ground was easy, and we clambered up gently sloping slabs covered with broken rock. Lucien and Robert led here, as they had covered this ground on their first reconnaissance of the Spur. Well knowing my friends, I made the following suggestion: "Now, no racing, or you'll only get out of breath and pack up."

The easy terrain, coupled with our desire to break fresh ground, was deceptive, for although our speed was quite moderate, it was still too great, and the height forced us to slow down.

We had ascended scarcely 60 feet before I found my heart pumping like that of an animal caught in a trap. My breathing became completely out of control. I had no time to exhale, for my lungs urgently demanded the already rarefied oxygen.

I stopped, and the sensation of suffocation lasted for some time after I had done so, then the rhythm became more normal.

I started off again, and 30 feet higher the same process was repeated. Each time I stopped I felt exactly as one does at the finish of a ski race, when one falls over in trying desperately to get one's breath. I wanted to ask the others if they felt the same, but I hadn't the courage. However, in spite of all this, we were gaining height, and soon left the crest of the Spur and bore off to the right towards the couloir below the Rock Wall underneath the Middle Glacier.

Lucien, 100 feet higher up, was already coping with the smooth rocks in the couloir. He turned round and called out to me:

"You see that corner. It's the only place where we might be exposed to falling séracs or stones, so keep a good look-out, and hurry."

I nodded my head as a sign that I understood and chuckled to myself: "Hurry! It's as much as I can do to go on as I am. Nothing doing; I won't hurry. Anyhow, it is well known that the stones always fall to one side!"

Keeping a sharp look-out, we climbed the couloir without incident—all that happened was that two or three large stones came down about 40 feet away and disappeared over the avalanche cone.

We left the couloir and ascended obliquely to the left by easy slabs leading again to the crest of the Spur. I caught up with Robert and Lucien, who were sitting waiting for me on some sunlit rocks.

"What about a rest?"

"All right. We'll stop here for a quarter of an hour; do you agree?"

I was quite ready to agree, and took off my sack. The simple fact of no longer having the straps on my shoulders gave immediate relief to my lungs, and I was glad to sit down on a rock.

This was the farthest point attained by the reconnaissance party. We could only see the next 150 feet or so, which looked easy. It consisted of fairly steep slopes of dirty scree, but higher up the Spur steepened, and it was not possible to see what followed. The short rest over, we started off again. We soon climbed up the scree slope, which, although easy, was troublesome, as we sank up to our ankles in the loose debris at every step. We scrambled up some broken rocks which led to a tiny

ROUND A CORNER APPEARED THE SOUTH FACE

Sommet Sud 6,982   Sommet Nord 7,035

6,000

5,000

4,000

SOUTH PEAK 22,900′, NORTH PEAK 23,075′
6000 m.=19,680′, 5000 m.=16,400′, 4000 m.=13,120′

ledge exactly above Camp I, and we could see below us the little yellow tent, which enabled us to form an idea of the height gained.

We looked up at the great cliff of brown rock above us. The narrow ledge on which we stood appeared to be the start of the difficult section.

I pulled a rope out of my sack and began to uncoil it.

"Good! Who's leading?" asked Lucien.

"As I've just got out this 170-foot rope, my sack is lighter, so I'll start," I replied.

"All right. Are you taking pitons?"

I looked up at the pitch ahead. It consisted of a fairly steep ridge with good holds ending in an overhang split by cracks.

"No, it's not worth it; it should 'go' without."

Lucien picked up the loops: "O.K.; carry on."

I started slowly up the ridge, taking care not to get out of breath. I treated the holds with caution, without exerting too much force: no pulling up with the arms, use the feet as much as possible, watch the balance. . . . I had soon climbed the ridge and reached the overhang.

With my legs wide apart and my body touching the rock, I examined the pitch. It was quite impossible to climb it direct, for the flakes of rock on which I had been counting were loose and broken. There was only one thing to do: traverse slightly to the right.

On this side, however, the ridge plunged downwards in a succession of almost vertical slabs to the avalanche cone of the right-hand couloir, 400 feet below. I should have to make a traverse of about 10 feet above this void, and in consequence my views on the subject of pitons underwent a radical change.

I turned to Lucien and said jauntily:

"You know I said it would 'go' without pitons. Well, I think, after all, I should like to put one in here on the right. . . . It's a bit sticky."

After a slight manipulation of the rope I quickly

retrieved three pitons, four karabiner and a hammer. At the second attempt the piton went in up to the ring, with a nice, clear, sound. Karabiner . . . rope. . . .

The traverse was successfully accomplished; the old familiar sound of steel on rock revived the joy of climbing. I found that I was actually smiling. Fifty feet below, Lucien was paying attention to the other end of the rope. It was safe to go on.

I balanced myself carefully on the slab, stretched across and landed slowly on my right foot; there were two cracks convenient for my hands. After a little shuffle to change feet, I rested for a moment and looked over towards the couloir, then, after standing upright, I was able to reach the edge of the small terrace. A short pull up, and I was there. I belayed Robert, who soon joined me.

"That was a nice bit of overhang!"

I replied, somewhat hypocritically: "Oh, just a small five." *

The conversation ended here, but it was of cardinal importance, for it was the first time we had climbed together, and from the gleam in Robert's eye I realised that our real friendship had begun at that moment.

Lucien climbed the pitch very quickly and joined us.

"Well, what now? Oh, that way. . . . Carry on; we'll follow."

While I had got my breath, Robert took over the lead and attacked the ensuing steep slab. This pitch was about 120 feet high and was split across the middle by a sort of saddle formed by a detached gendârme. Within the space of a few minutes the nature of the rock had completely changed; we had just passed through an area of sound fissured rock—something like the granite found

---

* Pitch of the fifth degree in the scale of difficulties which ranges from I to VI, the latter being considered as the extreme limit of possibility.

in the Alps—and now we came to an entirely different type of strata. The rock, grey in colour, was very broken up, with small and crumbling holds. It resembled badly mixed concrete—something we had never encountered previously.

Robert advanced extremely slowly, with great attention to balance. It was quite impossible to knock in pitons, as the rock simply broke away in pieces. We fully realised that we were taking a great risk. Nobody said a word. At last he reached the saddle and sat astride it.

"Oh Lord! everything's rotten; nothing stays put. You have to use the holds without knowing whether they are going to come away in your hand. What a business!"

I now climbed the first part of the pitch and joined Robert on the saddle. After considerable acrobatic manœuvres we managed to change places and he started off again.

What followed was not very encouraging. There was no doubt whatever that everything was loose. I had unpleasant proof of this in the form of small pieces of displaced rock sent down by Robert, who was obliged to do some "gardening" with his hammer in order to get down to the "solid" rock. As I was unable to move, I had to endure with fortitude the hail of missiles which this work entailed.

At long last he reached the top of the slab. We were now all together on a small ledge, which we enlarged by throwing some boulders into the couloir. We took stock of our position: there was little doubt that we would have to provide these two pitches with fixed ropes, and even with their help it was going to be a slow job ferrying the loads necessary for the establishment of higher camps.

It was already one o'clock, so, after nibbling some dried fruit and a little nougat, we started off again.

We traversed across the flank of a rounded rock tower and arrived at the foot of a big rock couloir. We were rather baffled by the terrain in general, which was like nothing we had ever seen before. Even the configuration of the rocks and the shape and size of the towers and couloirs were unfamiliar.

The couloir resembled one half of a concrete pipe, widening out at the top, and disappearing at the foot of a sort of buttress with a very steep and rounded crest. Now, for the first time, we could see a long way ahead, and were considerably disconcerted by the bleak, almost lunar aspect of these grey, lifeless rocks, completely without colour and looking rather like an unhealthy, dried-up skin. Further on, the Spur reared up and split up into several towers about 130 feet high. They were almost vertical, and looked very menacing. Above these towers a formidable cliff about 260 feet high soared upwards to join the Middle Glacier.

We gazed in silent contemplation at this not very encouraging sight. We had hoped to find a site for a camp on rounding the tower, but there was no indication whatever of any level ground.

Lucien remarked: "It's not very late; let's go on for a couple of run-outs. You never know, we might come across an unexpected ledge."

He started leading up the big couloir; meanwhile we had been able to hammer in a piton at the angle of the tower. He made good progress up the lower part of the couloir, which was not very steep; 60 feet higher it widened out and disappeared into the face. Standing on minute holds, Lucien made a rapid survey:

"How much slack?"

"Oh, you can go on; there's about half left."

"That's good. It's lousy; everything's rotten."

I interjected: "Put in a piton from time to time; we can't belay you very well."

I received a vague grunt in reply. He ascended a few feet more and then spent a good five minutes putting in a big piton. He was making slow but regular progress: from below we could see him zig-zagging from right to

88

left, which didn't seem to make sense, as conditions in the couloir looked all the same to us.

There were no cracks or projections of any sort, only a smooth surface with finger- and toe-holds, demanding delicate balance. At the end of the run-out he inserted two pitons, and we climbed the 200-foot pitch in our turn. There was practically no stance at all, so I enlarged it slightly with a few judicious hammer-blows. Lucien went on. 130 feet above, a small bulge broke the monotony of the wall, and on this he took a stance. We followed him and were once more together. Lucien and Robert were sitting astride it when I arrived, and there was no room for me. I was obliged to rest a few feet below with my feet on tiny holds, and could keep into the rock only by firmly grasping Robert's ankle. Lucien was determined to go "just a little higher". About a rope's length ahead we could just see the tips of some ice pinnacles, which suggested that there might be room there for a tent. I was sceptical, but Lucien had already started. I got on to the bulge beside Robert, and from this most uncomfortable position we slowly paid out the rope to Lucien, who was making quite good progress, sweeping off the loose stones as he went. He finally scaled a small, crumbling bluff and reached the pinnacles.

"Well?"

"Nothing doing. There's only a few square inches of level ground, and further on it's terrible. There's a whole series of chimneys leading down to the Great Couloir."

"But what about a tent? Any hopes?"

"Not a sausage. You've no idea what it's like from down there: there's nothing but holes!"

Robert and I exchanged glances. It was already half-past three, and we did not know how long it would take us to get back to our tent. We should have to rappel the whole way down, and to do that we needed sound rock in which to knock pitons. At all costs we must begin to think about descending. Lucien's voice floated down to us: he still wanted to go another rope's length higher, as he thought he could see a possible terrace. We strongly opposed this and said quite firmly that we had done enough for one day.

"Come down."

After a little argument Lucien agreed and turned to descend.

"How are you coming down? By rappel?"

"No, it would take too long; I'll come down free."

Silence. We looked at the pitch. It was not very steep, but there was a hundred feet of it, and we could not put in a piton to make a belay. If he slipped we should have our work cut out to catch him. Lucien explained what he proposed to do.

"Now, look; I'm coming down facing out, and braking with my hands and feet. If I do come off, I'll try to fall over to your right. O.K.?"

There was nothing to say to this. Tensed up, we watched him slide down amidst a small avalanche of stones; a last glissade, and he was with us. We heaved a sigh of relief.

Two rappels of 200 feet took us back to the start of the big pitch up which Robert had led earlier on. We decided to deal with this at once, and fixed a rope round a boulder, which we left hanging. A further rappel past a jammed and rather loose block took us down to the top of the Spur, and after a few feet of climbing along its crest we attained the scree slope, down which we ran in great strides. We quickly reached the couloir, and a few minutes later were back in Camp I.

The relief party had arrived, and Adrien, Pierre and Edmond plied us with questions.

We were surprised not to see Réné with the others, and Edmond said that he had a touch of lumbago.

"It took him very suddenly last night on the glacier, and this morning he couldn't move. He is bent double, and his leg hurts a lot."

I tried to get details, but Edmond was unable to tell
me much more.

"Anyhow," he said, "you'll know soon enough: you're
the doctor. I just don't know; he can't move and is in
pain, and that's that."

We talked it over, and finally we all decided to go
down, for it was no good leaving three men at Camp I.
We had learned from our experience of the night before
that the tent was not big enough for three, and moreover
there was plenty of stuff still to bring up. In the end
Adrien and Pierre remained, while Edmond went down
with us. We explained in some detail the route which
we had followed: tomorrow they would have to go up
very lightly equipped—just taking ropes to fix at the
places indicated by us. We descended very quickly to
Base Camp, which we reached at half-past seven, pretty
tired. Réné was waiting for us at the entrance to the
tent and, as Edmond had said, was doubled up like an
old man. He came forward to meet us with some
difficulty.

"Well, what's it like up there?"

"And what's the matter with you?"

"It's my beastly back: I can't move. I hope it's going
to work out all right. What about the Spur? Is it practicable?"

We gave him a detailed description of what we had
done, but were unable to predict what we were likely to
meet with higher up. All we could say was that the Spur
was difficult, even more difficult than we had expected.
On the other hand, there did not appear to be any
insuperable technical difficulty on this part of the Face.
We were of the opinion that we could scale the first
gendârmes and reach the base of the Great Towers,
which in itself would be a considerable achievement, for,
as we explained to Réné, there was no doubt that when
tackling this portion of the Spur we would have to be
provided with fixed ropes to facilitate the ferrying of

loads. Once at the base of the Great Towers, we had no idea whether we would be able to force them. It was essential to do so, for they barred the way to the Middle Glacier, which we had to reach if we were to go on at all. These towers therefore formed the key to the ascent of the Spur, and unfortunately were situated on the top part. We were all agreed on one thing, and that was that, having surmounted them, we would have overcome the first and most important pitch on the Face, and we were convinced that the remaining part of the climb would not produce anything quite so critical. We could talk of nothing else during our evening meal. At half-past nine we exchanged the light signals with Camp I, but did not keep this up for long, and soon withdrew to the warmth of our tents. We were very tired, but completely relaxed, and were able to slide into our sleeping-bags with an absolute sense of security and well-being. We had come down from the front line to base, well out of range of the mountain. No longer did we keep an ear open for the sound of stones ricocheting down the couloirs or the roar of an avalanche. We were able to abandon ourselves to the luxury of a deep and peaceful sleep.

Next day was like a Sunday. We did not get up until ten o'clock, and then only in *déshabille*. We blinked in the sunlight and took a quick look through our glasses. Adrien and Pierre were already high up the Spur. After breakfast we decided the time had come to do something about our appearance, for we had not had a really proper wash for ten days. When we had washed and shaved we were so pleased with ourselves that we decided to immortalise this great moment by photography.

A little later Lieutenant Ramazzi arrived with a column of mules, and in a trice the camp assumed the atmosphere of a fair: clouds of dust, shouts from the soldiers urging the mules up the last steep ascent, sounds of boots on rocks and the metallic tinkling of the loads.

The caravan had brought mail, the first instalments of the prefabricated hut to be erected on the site of our Base Camp, meat, fresh vegetables and wine. We ourselves off-loaded the precious bottles from the mule, not trusting such valuable cargo to any possible clumsiness on the part of the soldiers. Lucien became almost lyrical and in a few well-chosen words intoned a song of praise to mules in general, especially to those which carried wine! Our lunch was a very convivial affair, for the wine, together with the altitude, produced a slight sense of intoxication, so that by the end of the meal we had virtually conquered the Face.

We could still see Adrien and Pierre, who had got as far as our highest point. We guessed from their slowness and frequent halts that they were placing fixed ropes. In order to take our minds off the Face, Lucien, Edmond and I saddled three mules and went for a long ride alongside the glacier. Adrien and Pierre arrived back in camp at half-past six, showing signs of hard work and much sunburn. They took off their sacks, sat down on the edge of the terrace, elbows on knees, and gave a classic impression of athletes in repose.

"Well, we've done the job."

We thought it was time to say our little piece.

"Have you heard *our* news?"

"What?"

"The provisions have arrived . . . including some wine."

At once the lounging figures sat up straight, and their heads turned as one in the direction of the speaker. An expansive smile appeared on Adrien's face, and Pierre lost his usual *blasé* expression. A bottle was produced, and ten minutes later it was empty. Their fatigue had suddenly disappeared, and Adrien gave us a report of their activities with such incredible loquacity that we were completely unable to ask any questions, struck dumb by the unceasing flow of words.

The evening meal was a gay one, for we were once again reunited, and everybody had his say. Like us, Adrien and Pierre could not sleep peacefully at Camp I: they experienced the same sensations as we did, and asked each other the same questions concerning the possibility of avalanches. The conversation got gayer and gayer, interspersed with questions and cross-examinations. Fresh bottles of wine were opened under the slightly disapproving eye of Réné, and when the meal was finished Robert suggested opening his famous bottle of "firewater", usually kept for great occasions. There was no excuse whatever for doing so, but as we reserved the right to decide what was an "occasion", we opened it without more ado. I do not know whether it was the height or the brandy, but whatever it was had a most soporific effect, for that night we slept as never before, to the accompaniment of beautiful dreams.

We took the next morning very gently. Adrien was feeling slightly under the weather, and some of us, a little maliciously, attributed this to our libations of the previous night. Whatever it was, he was tired and feverish.

"The altitude, of course," chaffed Lucien, with a meaning smile.

As I took my job as M.O. of the party seriously, I made him describe his symptoms in detail, which, I must say, had much in common with those usually experienced "the morning after". However, the height has a peculiar physiological effect on the human body, so, to make quite certain, I prescribed a light diet and copious draughts of *mil hombres*—so called because this Argentine potion is said to have cured thousands of men. My reasoning was that if it had cured so many, why should it not have the same result with Adrien? The fact remains that by the evening he had quite recovered, but in his opinion the same result could have been obtained with hot wine!

After lunch we got ready the loads for the party going up to Camp I later in the afternoon. Towards three o'clock the weather began to break up, banks of cloud spread from the Pacific, closed round the summit and slowly descended the Face in long streamers, finally levelling off at about 18,000 feet. In view of this we postponed the start and wandered about in a rather disconsolate manner. Fortunately we discovered a pleasant way of passing the time, thanks to the soldiers of our supply column. This was pistol and mauser shooting. For more than an hour the mountain walls resounded to the crack of firearms, and numerous bottles strategically placed on neighbouring rocks were sacrificed for a Franco–Argentine shooting contest. We finished the afternoon by playing chess and canasta, and about 6 p.m. the temperature dropped and the sky gradually cleared. Before long the Face became visible once more and we could see the tops of the mountains covered with fresh snow. The sunset was a fine one, and promised good weather for the morrow.

February 4th

It was a beautiful day, and far away down the valley a few filmy clouds were floating in the calm air, for all the world like those seen in travel advertisements. We left camp at three o'clock—Robert, Lucien, Edmond and I— with very heavy loads, reaching Camp I at a quarter past five, having improved on our previous time for the climb. We made another platform for the second tent which we had taken with us. This took two hours of hard work, for we were obliged to break stones out of the Face to acquire building material. Edmond sarcastically remarked that if this sort of thing was going to happen regularly it would have been much better to have brought some professional navvies with us, rather than climbers. "All I have done up to now is to carry heavy loads and hump rocks and stones." As soon as the tent was up, Robert, who was not lacking in ideas, suggested installing the cooker at once. This we did by constructing a miniature terrace surrounded by a little wall, in the middle of which Robert placed the cooker with a self-satisfied smirk. After the usual exchange of signals with Base Camp we settled down for the night. We now had two tents for two men each—a much better arrangement, giving us a great deal more room all round. In spite of this comparative comfort and warmth, I did not succeed in having a really good night. Although I was getting used to it, I still felt slightly anxious, as on the first night —probably I would never be able to sleep comfortably at Camp I.

We left next morning at about 9 a.m., despite protests from Robert, who had been up since eight o'clock and kept complaining about our slow start. He said I was a "fat slug", but I told him that for many years I had had a particular aversion from the early morning freshness of the mountains. Our sacks were very heavy, and we made many halts before we reached the first pitch, with the fixed rope put there by Adrien and Pierre. We decided to replace it with a looped rope, for, as we would have to climb it more than once with heavy sacks, it would "go" much better like this than with a plain rope. Loops for the hands would make the pitch much easier and safer, for we were climbing unroped, in order to save time. All the pitches in the grey couloir were now equipped with fixed ropes: Adrien and Pierre had certainly not wasted their time. I derived considerable encouragement from their labours, for it was very pleasant to see a piton already in position with a rope attached to it. I acquired renewed confidence as I went on; I saw that we could completely rely on one another in every respect. Our characters might be different, but we regarded the technical problems with a common eye, and it did not matter in the least who had fixed the ropes or knocked in the pitons.

We were spread out along the whole length of the big grey couloir, like spiders on the same thread. Robert and Lucien had got to the saddle. We all stopped here and attached ourselves to the ropes by karabiner. Lucien then went on, and finally reached the point he had got to the last time. Robert then went up in his turn, and I took his place astride the saddle. I was extremely gratified to notice the two enormous pitons (broches) holding the 600 feet of rope which we had placed in position. Higher up, the others were already fixing the next rope. Edmond now took my place, while I went up and joined Lucien, who was belaying Robert in the lead. The next run-out took him to a ledge at the base of the Little Towers. It was now time to make a decision as to the next move. The Face steepened above us, and we could see no sign of a site for even one tent. We were now much nearer to the Great Towers about 500 feet above us. They still looked most formidable, and we had no idea how we were going to deal with them. For want of a better site we decided to leave some equipment for a future Camp II where we were and attached to two pitons a sack containing two sleeping-bags, a gas cooker with enough fuel for ten hours, some food, two axes and two pairs of crampons. While we were sorting all this out, Edmond climbed still higher and fixed our last 200-foot rope. He came down very pleased at having got further up the Face than anybody else.

We returned to Camp I by the simple process of sliding down the fixed ropes, taking all precautions, however, as we were not belayed in any way, and this first "solitary" descent made a considerable impression on us. We had gained a great deal of time on our first descent, and after a slight rest at Camp I we reached the glacier by 6 p.m. We met Pierre and Adrien on the moraine. They had started late from camp, preferring to go up in the cool of the evening. We told them all we knew, and advised them to take as much rope as possible, as it was more than likely that we should have to fix ropes up the rest of the Spur. Our two parties went on their separate ways, they bound for hard work and possible danger, while we descended rapidly towards the peace and quiet of Base Camp.

Chapter Two

THE FIGHT FOR CAMP II

Base Camp, February 6th

WE had got used to these rest days, and made the most of them. We wandered about the camp, untidy, dirty, doing our best to avoid the least amount of work and arguing about the slightest thing. The toss of a coin decided who should boil the water for breakfast; the loser would have his bread buttered by the next one in the work queue, and while the third was doling out the breakfast drink into the mugs, the fourth would criticise until he was told off by the other three "workers". We set up a sort of observation post, with the telescope permanently trained on the Spur. A large tin served as a chair, and in this way we were able to maintain a satisfactory watch on the Face. One of us was always on watch, while the rest lounged in the sun, hats over their eyes and constantly demanding an action report.

It was eleven o'clock, and Adrien and Pierre were making slow progress up the fixed ropes. It was easy to guess, from their pace and frequent halts, that they were heavily loaded. By 1 p.m. they were above the place where we had dumped the equipment. After about half an hour's rest we saw them begin to descend without sacks. This retreat was received with a volley of abuse, and I am sure that their ears must have been burning.

Our peevishness was assuaged when we saw them stop at Camp I, for we then realised that they must have been overloaded and, feeling tired, had decided to go up again the next day to continue the work. This was obviously

99

the case, for they slept at Camp I, and we received the usual signal from them that night.

Next morning we saw them at the equipment dump and watched their progress above the point which we had reached two days before. Thanks to their coloured anoraks, we could see them quite easily, and noted that they were leading through. They went straight up to the base of the Little Towers, then traversed to the right and started up a sort of curving chimney. We were able to see that they were fixing ropes as they went along. Having reached the top of the chimney, they then attacked the top part of one of the towers by its arête. From below this pitch looked absolutely vertical, and we were intrigued to see these two figures clinging to this forbidding wall. Another run-out and they were at the top of the Little Towers. Nice work; they had certainly made great progress up the long route leading to the Middle Glacier. We could not tear ourselves away from the telescope, and awaited the sequel with interest. They were now close to the foot of the Great Towers. Would they find a site there for Camp II, or would they have to go on? We could not quite make out what they were doing, for when they both reached the top of their tower they sat down, and remained there for a long time. What on earth were they doing? They were still there two hours later. We hadn't a clue, but this inexplicable delay did not seem to us to be a good omen. Finally, at five o'clock, they started to descend just as we were setting out for Camp I.

These starts for the Face were now well organised and had become a matter of routine. We always took a pack-mule loaded with our sacks as far as the bottom of the great central névé, as a pretext for avoiding the fatigue of carrying them over the level moraine. Mercedes accompanied us, and we started off in shirt sleeves, like tourists. Ice-axe under the arm, we peacefully followed the mule, which stumbled over débris of ice and stones. This pleasant

THE BASE OF THE CENTRAL SPUR. TENTS OF CAMP I AT 14,435', IN
SMALL CIRCLE

CENTRAL SPUR ABOVE CAMP I UP TO CAMP III. GREAT TOWERS INDICATED
BY THE CROSS

interlude was unfortunately only too short, and ceased at the foot of the névé. Here we took leave of Mercedes. "Well, *hasta mañana*, we'll be down tomorrow."

He smiled all over his sunburned face and wished us good luck. He said a lot more which we could not understand, but we guessed that he wished he were coming with us. We invariably took about five minutes to say good-bye to him, for he and his mule represented creature comforts, whereas 100 feet higher began our hard labour. We had no sooner left him than we found ourselves in another world, bounded by mountains and governed by different physical and metaphysical laws with which we had to contend if we wished to exist at all. We reached Camp I with relief, and Robert said that we had improved on our time—an hour and a half from Base Camp, which was less than half the time taken for the first ascent. There was no doubt that we were getting acclimatised and were in good training. Adrien and Pierre had not yet arrived, but we knew they would not be long, for a cloud of red dust indicated that they were glissading down the scree slope above the couloir. They joined us within a quarter of an hour.

"Well! Come on, what's happened?"

Adrien replied after getting his breath: "We've fixed ropes to the top of the Little Towers."

"We know that; but what about Camp II? Have you found a site?"

"Not a hope; couldn't even put up one tent."

"Well, then, higher up."

"There was nothing to be seen higher up."

"Well, what have you been doing? We saw you resting for two hours. Can we get beyond the Great Towers?"

We kept plying them with questions, for we were anxious to know the worst. It seemed extraordinary to us that there was no suitable site, for from below it looked as though it must be possible to put one somewhere. Pierre let us go on talking and then said:

"You'll see for yourselves tomorrow. You say you saw us sitting down? There was just room for two close together. It's exactly like lower down, arête following arête, and couloirs; only they are all much steeper. There's not more than about a square foot of flat ground."

Adrien, the optimist, said that higher up perhaps . . . but they couldn't say anything definite.

"But," said Lucien, "you got to the foot of the Great Towers; you saw them. Can one climb them?"

Pierre merely smiled, and Adrien, wishing to tell us something concrete, said: "I think they'll 'go', but I can't guarantee it. Anyway, you'll see tomorrow."

They went down, leaving us alone with our thoughts and the dirty dishes. Lucien assumed an attitude of injured innocence, Edmond couldn't care less, while Robert, who was nothing if not practical, said why not wash up? Faced by this impasse, Lucien went in search of water. He soon came back saying, "There's not a drop anywhere, except perhaps in the Great Couloir; and anyhow it's not my turn."

We seized the dishes and trooped off in the direction of the couloir. A rapid glance showed us what Lucien meant. Water was cascading from the bottom of a patch of snow—easy enough to reach across about thirty feet of smooth slabs, but very exposed to falling stones and ice. This couloir, which came straight down from the Middle Glacier, was a regular channel for anything falling from above. We watched for some minutes, but nothing fell.

Lucien contrived to get out of this job by offering to act as look-out. Robert and I went off to fill the dishes by putting them under the little waterfall, while Lucien never took his eyes off the overhanging séracs above. After what seemed an age, the dishes were full and we returned to camp, taking great care not to spill any of the precious water.

February 8th

By dawn the clouds which had veiled the North Arête the previous night had disappeared. It was a lovely day, and I took advantage of it by filming scenes in camp. We left at eight o'clock—much earlier than usual. As we were only carrying our climbing gear and fairly light sacks, I took my camera and made some shots on the Spur. We derived great assistance from the fixed ropes, and made such rapid progress that by 11 a.m. we reached the spot where Adrien and Pierre had stopped the previous day. We now fully understood their hesitation in expressing a definite opinion. We were at the foot of the Great Towers and at a height of over 16,400 feet, about 2,000 feet above Camp I with not the slightest sign of a ledge anywhere. We were advancing à cheval along the crest of the shattered ridge as well as we could, taking great precautions, in view of the rotten nature of the rock. Below a couloir cut across the Face obliquely to the right in the direction of the ice-fall of the Middle Glacier. We could see a pile of broken ice to the right of the 250-foot vertical wall immediately above us, which merged into the Face to our left in smooth slabs, plunging down to the Great Central Couloir.

The task ahead of us was quite obvious—indeed, brutally so. To attain the glacier we had either to turn this formidable wall or climb it direct.

Lucien suggested having a look into the couloir to see if it were possible to traverse to the right towards the ice-fall. I was not enthusiastic, but it was only logical to do so before attempting the direct ascent. He festooned himself with pitons, karabiner and étriers. We let him down on the rope into the couloir, which he crossed at once. He inserted a piton, went down about 30 feet, and then started on an extremely delicate diagonal traverse in order to reach a rounded rock knob almost without holds. He shouted instructions to us, for his balance depended on the pull of the rope, aided by the push of his feet against the rocks.

I said to Robert: "It won't 'go'; he'll have to try the direct route to the left."

"You're telling me! Look at the acrobatics. Take loads up that? Not on your life!"

Lucien went on for a while and got to the other side of the rounded knob.

"Well!"

He was silent for a moment, and then said: "Nothing doing. I should have to go on for at least another hundred and fifty feet, and even then I don't know if I could get to the beastly glacier. And what's more I'm just below the ice; it's a death-trap. Take in slowly, I'm coming back."

In a short time he rejoined us.

"Right. I'll try to the left, shall I?"

There was nothing else to do. If we couldn't find some means of scaling the Great Towers, it would be a disaster. All the hard work of equipping the Spur would have been wasted and the success of the whole venture jeopardised. We felt that the next few feet were critical. Lucien tackled a very steep slab which partly concealed an enormous, deep-cut crack. Reaching the top, he paused, out of breath, and looked at the huge fissure. The eternal question was asked once more, a little dolefully this time:

"Well, will it 'go'?"

He did not reply at once, but inspected the pitch as if the rock could supply him with the answer. He weighed the pros and cons before turning round:

"It's damned difficult, but we'll have to risk it. I think it will 'go'."

Robert started up like a gun-dog let off the lead.

"Good! Take in. I'm coming up to you and going to have a crack at it."

I paid out while he climbed the slab and joined

Lucien. Both men dived into their sacks and produced "the works", that is to say the whole armoury of pitons and étriers. At last Robert was ready. Belayed by the doubled rope, he started off, slowly mounting a very steep slab. After inserting a piton as belay, he continued up towards the foot of the chimney. The slab steepened and then overhung; he was now only a few feet from the chimney. He knocked in a piton at arm's length, snapped in a karabiner and attached an étrier to it, then, hanging by one hand to the étrier, he swung over to the left.

"It'll 'go', but it's no joke. . . . You jolly well know that you're 16,000 feet up. . . . I'm all out of breath. . . . I'm going to rest for a minute. . . ."

He puffed and blew for a while and then said:

"Right, I'm going on."

Once more he swung on the étrier, and at last got into the chimney. The rope ran out, then stopped; hammer-blows, the piton singing as it bit into the rock—a nice, clean, metallic sound. Lucien and I exchanged a glance; it was going well. After a slight pause:

"Slack, please. That's right, take in. Hold it. Pay out carefully; I'm going on."

The doubled rope ran out once again; more hammer-blows, and Robert came to view on a sort of step jutting out from the left wall of the chimney.

"I'm making a stance here."

"What's it like above?"

"There's a sort of inner chimney; it'll 'go'."

Robert took in the rope and Lucien joined him on the step. He stopped for a while, panting, then led through. He was now invisible to me, and the only sound was the echo of hammer-blows from the depths of the chimney. His voice was scarcely audible, the only words I could distinguish were short staccato orders for the manipulation of the rope. Suddenly a single sentence was heard, vibrant like a clarion call:

"That's it; I'm up!"

I tried to pick him out, but all I could see was Robert glued to the wall on his tiny stance, 100 feet above me. All at once Lucien appeared at the top, standing out against the sky. He uttered cries of joy and waved his arms about like a mechanical doll. Edmond was 60 feet below me, and could not see anything. He bombarded me with agitated questions:

"Well, is he up? Tell me where he is. Blast it! I can't see a thing. What's going on up there?"

There he was at the top of the Towers at last, most likely on an adequate terrace, for which we had been waiting for so long. Robert got impatient:

"Lucien, have you found somewhere for the tents?"

"No, nothing here; but perhaps higher up . . ."

Our spirits fell again, though by now we were getting used to the same reply, repeated daily, run-out after run-out; "Perhaps higher up"! We had made so certain this time that we felt we had been done down. We were entitled to a terrace, and there must be one somewhere on the Face. I was beginning to get really angry with the mountain, which seemed to be cheating. Robert's voice recalled me from my somewhat bitter thoughts:

"Lulu, what are we going to do?"

"Wait until we get a bit higher up. Anyhow, we've got to rope this pitch: you must bring up some rope."

"O.K. Shall I bring Guy up?"

"No, that's not necessary—just tell him to send up some more rope. It's too late to go any higher; we must just rope the Towers."

I unroped, and Robert pulled up the 200-foot rope on to which we had been tied. Edmond and I were now alone, separated from our two friends, so I joined him 60 feet lower down. We drove in a piton and attached to it everything still in our sacks—pitons, karabiner, rope slings and 100 feet of alpine line. As there was nothing more we could do, we started to go down, in order to save time, and about 60 feet lower down waited for them

to catch us up. Now that we were not so directly underneath, we could see them at work on the Great Towers.
Robert was in the act of climbing the second chimney,
while Lucien, who seemed to have nothing better to do,
was shouting at us. We couldn't hear a word he said,
but from the general intensity of his remarks we gathered
that they were insulting! While waiting for them we
made some Ovo, for we were extremely thirsty. Meanwhile our friends had fixed the ropes and were coming
down, preceded by an avalanche of small stones, some
of which came too near to be pleasant.

"Look out up there!" shouted Edmond.

"It's all right for you; all you've got to do is to sit
pretty."

I replied in the same strain of doubtful humour:

"Oh, don't worry about us, but the dish of Ovo which
we're making for you is . . ."

The avalanche died away at once, and our friends
shouted that they would do all they could not to disturb
the smallest pebble. Perched together on our rock, we
quaffed our drink. The Towers were conquered, everybody was optimistic—a job well done. Edmond made a
noise like a siren: "Hoo, hoo, the old firm of the South
Face has closed down. Everybody out. Nobody works
overtime nowadays."

We got ready for the descent, which we had brought to
a fine art. We put on our anoraks and leather gloves, so
as not to burn our hands and backs. The first man
seized the rope, put it round his thighs and, with his
arms extended, supported himself on it like a boxer at
rest in his corner. He then let himself slide down, face
outwards, at the same time walking down the wall with
his feet. He could regulate the speed of the descent by
alternately grasping and releasing the rope with his
hands. (*Translator's Note:* This must be an error. Face
outwards instead of inwards would be a most un-
orthodox, if not impossible, method of descent.) We

descended without belays: as soon as one of us had passed a piton, the next man started sliding down in his turn, and in this manner we went down the whole 1,300 feet in little more than half an hour.

We reached Base Camp at about 8 p.m., and were received by the others with enthusiasm. Réné, Pierre and Adrien had watched us through their glasses, and were full of congratulations for our conquest of the lower part of the Face, thus opening the way to the Middle Glacier.

I found Réné very tired and with a lined face. He said he could not sleep, for the pain gave him no respite. It had gone from his back down to his right leg and he could not rest in any one position for more than a few minutes. He told me that he had tried everything, and during the last two days had taken any medicine he could get hold of which held out the slightest hope of curing rheumatic disorders.

"I'm browned off," he concluded. "If I don't get better soon I'm going to Inca. Just look at me, I'm crawling along like an old man; can't even lace up my boots, and all I have to do all day is to get bored. I hear Dr. Antinucci is coming up here; I only hope he can do something about it."

I was very glad to hear that a real doctor was on the way, for I felt quite incapable of helping Réné. We turned our evening meal into a banquet in celebration of the forcing of the Towers. There were no actual speeches, but everyone seemed to talk without stopping. A feeling of optimism had set in, and we all were agreed that the worst was over.

"Just think," said someone, "all this artificial climbing at over 16,000 feet. In my opinion today was the crux of the climb. We've won through."

"Don't forget that there is still the Rock Wall; but it should go all right, for the rock is of much better quality."

"After which come the séracs; but one can always get through them, and once on the Upper Glacier there are no more difficulties."

Everyone was happy and confident. At the end of the meal Robert's bottle of brandy was produced, the contents of which were sadly diminished when we broke up early next morning. The night was cold when we turned in, and clouds covered the Face, but we were not discouraged. Everyone got into his sleeping-bag thinking of the victory to come.

Next morning we awoke in a grey, diffused light. Through the tent door we could see that the Face was plastered with new snow, clouds were tearing across the crests and their base was very low. We were not unduly disturbed at the sight of this snow; today was an off day, anyhow, so we were quite prepared to let the mountain indulge if it so desired.

By midday, however, the weather had got worse and the cloud-base was lower—right down to the glacier, in fact. Before long the camp itself was affected, and it began to snow heavily, covering the tents with a thick layer. The temperature had fallen suddenly to below freezing point. Everyone was immobilised; some wrote letters or slept, others played cards or chess. The day passed very slowly, and we retired early, hoping for an improvement on the morrow.

February 10th

It was a cold night. Through the cloud-breaks we could see a completely white Face. This was the first time we had encountered a really bad weather cycle and were not prepared for it. At eleven o'clock Dr. Antinucci arrived from Puente del Inca, and his visit cheered us up enormously. The doctor literally oozed optimism, and was very glad to have the opportunity of speaking French once more.

"You must tell your friends when you get back to

France that in Argentina the doctor pays his visits by mule instead of by car."

He had made a six-hour trip by mule in order to examine Réné, who was no better. His diagnosis was fairly pessimistic, the height, the cold and the conditions of camp life were doing him no good at all. He would have to go down if he wanted to be completely cured. Réné wouldn't hear of it.

"Nothing doing. You'll have to think up something else, doctor."

The doctor shook his head. "All right, then I'll have to try injections."

Réné made a face and looked at me—he had a horror of injections, syringes and the like.

I fully sympathised, sharing his objections, but for want of anything better I advised him to submit to the treatment. While we were getting the injection ready, Lucien came in.

"Here you are, Guy; there's something for you."

He held out a bleeding hand, with a deep cut in the left index finger.

"Cutting ham," he said in reply to our questions—"the knife slipped."

Fortunately I was able to turn the case over to our professional, and acted as assistant while the doctor bound the finger up. Réné's injections finished the sick parade, and then it was time for lunch, after which the doctor went back to Inca, with the intention of returning the next day. We were full of admiration of the manner in which he took in his stride all these repeated journeys on mule-back, twenty miles each way over the bad track between here and Inca.

An hour later the snow began to fall again in big flakes which showed no sign of stopping; it was most discouraging. We retired to the big mess tent and resumed the inevitable games of canasta. At 8 p.m. it slackened off, and finally stopped. There was over a foot of snow on the tents, which caused the poles to bend in an alarming manner, so we set to work to brush it off before damage was done. The clouds, blown apart by the night wind, revealed shreds of livid sky. The mountains seemed to have come closer, surrounding us with their oppressive whiteness. The skeleton of the partly erected refuge with its metal framework served to accentuate the impression of the bones of an antediluvian monster.

A feeling of deep sadness seemed to emanate from this dead landscape, enveloping us and penetrating into our very bones. Even the air we breathed seemed to have a bitter taste. We shivered, gripped by an icy cold, and had an absurd desire to cry.

Every now and again the Face showed itself, revealing fantastic precipices draped with curtains of ice. Huge avalanches broke away from it, shattering the intense silence with loud rumblings. The snow coming from above was collected by the couloirs and carried down to the glacier, where it spread out like a wave breaking on a groin. Spellbound, we watched the savage spectacle, swathed in our anoraks. Nature was displaying its elemental strength, and we suddenly realised how impotent we were before these impressive manifestations.

Pierre expressed our innermost thoughts:

"Well, there's no doubt that takes the gilt off the gingerbread!"

"When I think we were up there," said Edmond; "just imagine being stuck up there in this."

Adrien said, pointing to the Face, "Just look there, through the gap in the clouds. See that ice-fall? It's terrific. It must be at least 500 feet."

"Sometimes I begin to wonder if we haven't let ourselves in for something," said Robert. "Make no mistake, it's a bit out of our world; we aren't in the picture."

Lucien, who had said nothing up to now, immediately took another and more optimistic view:

"Now just a minute. Morale seems low this evening! I grant you the mountain is a bit of a basket, but even so it's only a mountain, like all the rest; and don't forget we've roped the whole of the Spur from top to bottom. Basket or not, we've met others; we've come here to collect its scalp, and we will—just like the rest. Aconcagua or no Aconcagua, it's only ice and rock, after all; and we can deal with that!"

This pulled us together, and we could not but agree with this profession of faith.

I could not, however, refrain from a somewhat wry witticism: "O.K. We'll get its scalp—unless it gets ours first!"

This remark finally reduced the tension, and we resumed our evening meal free from the spell cast by the grey skies.

Next morning the weather was much better and a pallid sun shone on the camp. The snow was melting, but the wind continued to chase clouds from the Pacific over the crests. We could see the whole of the Face now sheathed in ice, it resembled a vast tapestry suspended from a stormy sky. As though shaken by an invisible hand, it threw off avalanches continuously. Through the glasses we could see the two tents of Camp I, almost buried in the snow. They were still standing, if slightly askew. We subsequently found that about 2 feet of snow had fallen at Camp I, and there must have been somewhere between 3 and 4 feet above 20,000 feet. We were somewhat perturbed at this quantity of snow and the consequent loss of time involved in waiting for the Face to return to normal.

At eleven o'clock the mule supply column arrived in charge of Sergeant Darvitch. We also had guests: the indefatigable Dr. Antinucci had come up, accompanied by his son and a *gaucho*, and, what is more, a young and charming Argentine girl who was spending a holiday at the hotel at Inca, had also arrived with her father. The unexpected presence of a young girl unleashed a positive outburst of gallantry—eight weeks' growth of beard disappeared in a trice, and some of us even went so far as to put on clean shirts and sort out ties to go with them! Our midday meal included grilled steak cooked by the *gaucho*: a distinct improvement on tinned food.

The girl had the very romantic Christian name of Lauredane, which added to her charm. Everybody was delighted when we learned that she (and her father) proposed spending the night with us. Our sudden desire to play the host had quite taken our minds off meteorological problems. Towards the end of the afternoon Dr. Antinucci and his son, together with the *gaucho*, left for Inca, and we were able to admire the horsemanship of this boy of twelve years old. He bade us farewell, and at the same time made his mule rear up with a skill and control which showed that he must have started riding at an age when most European children would have been learning to walk. The evening passed quickly, and conversation took place half in French and half in Spanish, finishing off with the usual games of canasta and chess. We did not get to bed before half-past twelve.

While we were undressing we heard a low murmur of voices, and a few moments later Mercedes appeared in the door of the tent. He spoke to Suzanne in very rapid Spanish, not a word of which we could understand. Suzanne gave us a quick *résumé*. It appeared that about a week previously half a dozen soldiers had put up a camp lower down the moraine, where they were engaged in cutting stones for the wall of the new refuge. One of them had just arrived seeking help for one of his friends who had been thrown by his mule last night.

Suzanne added: "You know, Guy, you'll have to go down; after all, you're the expedition M.O.!"

The prospect of climbing out of my warm sleeping-bag just when I had got myself comfortable for the night was not attractive. Feeling very aggressive, I asked her to find the extent of his injuries. After a short colloquy, she turned to me and said:

"This is what he tells me. The man fell on a rock and has fractured his spine. They can't move him: he's in too much pain. You really will have to go."

This only served to strengthen my conviction.

"Listen, Suzanne. If his spine is really broken, it would be better to send for a priest. I couldn't cope with it; and anyhow I'm not a doctor!"

"If he's suffering too much, you'll have to finish him off!" said Lucien.

After discussing the matter from the point of view of humanity, the honour of France and the absolute necessity of succouring a human being in distress, Lucien and I dragged ourselves out of bed and dressed.

Meanwhile, Mercedes had saddled our two mules. The soldier who had come with the message stood silently alongside his mule, which was steaming in the cold night air. The beasts bucked and kicked when we mounted them.

"If they go on like this, it's going to be fine," said Lucien. "I've often taken part in mountain rescue work, but never on a mule. You must agree it's a bit unusual."

Adrien, who had not gone to bed, saw us off. "It's a pity there isn't another mule, I'd like to have gone with you."

He was obviously quite sorry at not being able to come along.

Mercedes asked us if we were ready.

"Si, si, vamos."

He let go the bridles and the mules started to rear, which we corrected by a few judicious kicks. We started down the steep path, which descended the slope in zigzags, our guide preceding us by about ten yards or so. The night, which was already dark, got quite impenetrable when we entered a thick mist alongside the glacier. All we could see were a few dim silhouettes. Now and again we encountered boulders emerging from the fog, which just as quickly disappeared, swallowed up in the gloom. We carried on in silence, lulled by the rhythmical clatter of hooves on rock. In vain we tried to find landmarks in the darkness, but we could see nothing tangible, even our guide was scarcely visible. I suddenly recalled an old Scandinavian legend, in which the King of the Mists was taking his captives to his kingdom, where they would be condemned to wander for ever, like phantoms in the fog.

We had been going for more than two hours when we suddenly came to a halt in a sort of hollow among the rocks. Why had we stopped here? It was not the camp? Had we lost the track? A wild idea occurred to me. Was it an ambush? I rode forward and prepared to defend myself, but when I caught up with the soldier, he only asked me for a light! There was no doubt that this frolic was beginning to get on our nerves. Lucien must have thought the same, for his overwrought voice called out of the mist:

"Guy, where are you? What's going on? Good Lord! I can't see you now. Wait for me. My mule won't move."

When he caught up with us we tried to ask the soldier if it was a long way to the camp. So far as we could understand him, it was only a short distance. I took the lead and held Lucien's bridle so as to enable us to keep together. This did the trick, for I found that all I had to do was to give the mule his head, as he appeared to be following the invisible track without difficulty. Sometimes he would stop, stretch out his neck, prick up his ears like a radar aerial and then go on again. The instinct of these animals was as remarkable as their sureness of foot, for they were able to avoid large and quite invisible rocks. The sole disadvantage of this mode of progression was the pitching and tossing which it involved. This nocturnal rodeo was beginning to get me down, and just as the lights of the camp came in sight, I succumbed. Leaning miserably over the neck of my steed, I was horribly sick! What a come down! I had survived the sea and the air and had finished up by being mulesick! Fortunately the job in hand took my mind off such mundane matters. We went at once to see the injured man. After a rapid examination I was able to diagnose that he was suffering from nothing worse than a badly bruised back. I applied some neat alcohol to his bruises, despite his protestations, and then called it a day. The honour of France was saved, but it was already four o'clock in the morning, and much too late to think of returning the way we had come. We spent the night in a tent put at our disposal by the N.C.O. in charge.

Next morning we went back to Base Camp with the supply column. The journey which had seemed so long the night before was much quicker in the daylight. When we came to the crest of the moraine, the whole of the Face opened out before us and, being much further away from it than at Base Camp, we were able to form a better impression of its size. It was quite clear that we had climbed a good third of it. It was to be hoped that today's good weather would allow us to continue the assault. As we ascended, the patches of snow became more and more frequent, and when we arrived at Base Camp there was still far too much for our liking. In spite of the feeble sunshine we still hoped for better weather to come.

February 13th

Cloudy, with intermittent falls of snow. The Face was rumbling, continuously swept by huge avalanches. The day seemed endless, and we were very depressed by the return of the bad weather. For something to do, we decided to prepare a cooked meal. Edmond was the chief cook, and under his direction we busied ourselves in culinary preparations, consisting in the main in serving up the usual tinned food in an unusual way. Drawing

AFTER TEN DAYS OF BAD WEATHER, THE FACE LOOKED ANYTHING
BUT ENCOURAGING

THE GREAT TOWERS. LOADS ARE HAULED UP TO CAMP II OVER A 260′ SPAN

up the menu caused us rather a headache, and the only name we could think up for toad-in-the-hole was *hors d'œuvre variés*. The next course of meat was christened *sauté de veau, sauce Horcones*, the daily spaghetti was reborn as *spaghettis à la criollo*, the cheese became *fromages variés* and the *pièce de résistance*—Aconcagua cup—consisted of a tin of fruit topped with snow. This menu, written in pencil on small slips of paper placed before each diner, imparted a certain air of gastronomic well-being which helped us to forget our worries.

February 14th

It snowed the whole night, and this morning the weather was cloudy and threatening. We were at a complete loss for something to do, and in desperation, Adrien, Lucien and Pierre asked me to shave them—rather be cut than be bored to death! Snow fell intermittently throughout the day. We tried to relieve our frayed nerves by swearing, vying with each other to produce the most horrific words we could think of. We felt like prisoners in our stuffy tents. Would it never be fine again?

February 15th

The snow was sparkling under the rays of a warm, spring-like air; there were only a few clouds floating very high in the heavens and clinging for a moment or two to the topmost peaks before being carried further on by the wind. The signs indicated that the weather was on the mend, the air was lighter and more invigorating than hitherto, and we were glad to notice that the snow was melting and the Spur was gradually losing its mantle of white.

At midday a large caravan arrived in charge of our liaison officer, Lieutenant Ramazzi, in order to complete our new camp. A dozen soldiers had also come with

him, and would remain until it was finished. Dr. Antinucci was also with the party, accompanied by his
charming wife. She was so enraptured with our camp
that we invited them to stay with us for a few days.
Madame Antinucci was quite delighted with our invitation, which she immediately accepted.

"If this continues," said Lucien, "our camp is going to
become the fashionable rendezvous of all the summer
guests at Puente del Inca. 'What, you haven't been to the
French camp? But you must; it's terrific.'"

Edmond, with an eye to business, improved on this:

"No kidding, chaps, a good hotel, a night club with
band, and by day you can watch the French on the
South Face—the finest climb in the world. . . . See what
I mean!"

All this joking and general atmosphere of gaiety were
the external signs of a rise in our morale. We were all
bursting with suppressed energy, which had to have an
outlet somewhere. This thirst for action was demon-
strated during the afternoon in the form of a sort of
"briefing" such as pilots receive before the start of a war-
time mission. We arrived at certain definite conclusions.
It was quite obvious that we were dealing with no
ordinary mountain—we were faced with a problem entirely new judged by the usual alpine standards. What
we had to do was quite simple: reconcile the usual technique employed by expeditions in attempting a high
climb with the difficulties usually encountered on one of
the great alpine faces . . . and then multiply them by
three.

"You must remember," said Robert, "that we are not
operating under normal conditions. When an expedition
tries to conquer a peak of more than 23,000 feet, it usually
makes the attempt by the easiest route, whereas we're
going up the most difficult one, which is quite a different
kettle of fish."

Pierre broke in:

"You've also got to bear in mind that we've been 'working' on the mountain for the past three weeks and haven't yet established Camp II. If we go on like this, it'll take us another two years before we've put up the four camps necessary for victory—that is, if all goes well."

Everyone agreed with him, and Adrien summed up the situation:

"And there's another thing. We've had quite enough of these comings and goings; it's beginning to get us down. Each time we go up we think we're really going to get somewhere, and each time we're disappointed. We've had enough of that; it's time we adopted different methods."

"It's not difficult at all," said Lucien. "As soon as we've found somewhere to erect two tents, or even only one, we'll go on from there with everything on our backs in a dash for the summit. Just the old alpine technique; it's quite simple."

These two sentences expressed exactly what we all thought, and were received with exclamations of approval, interrupted by Réné:

"Quiet a moment, and listen to me. Unfortunately it doesn't concern me, for I can't move; but just listen. It was jolly good getting to the top of the Great Towers, but don't forget that there's still another 6000 feet to go to the summit. Go on by all means, but remember that if the weather breaks you run the risk of being stuck there. I'm all for pushing on, but not at any price. You don't know what you're likely to meet with up there, so don't get too involved and run too many risks."

Pierre, silent up to now, replied to Réné, putting forward views which we felt were carefully thought out:

"We all agree with you; after all, you're the leader, and it is only right that you should think dispassionately and act as a brake. . . ."

"I'm not blaming you," interjected Réné, with a

smile; "on the contrary, it's a good thing for an expedition leader to have to hold back his team. . . ."

Pierre went on: "I don't know what's in your minds, but I think Lucien's right. You needn't worry, we're not going to rush it like lunatics. We've just got to think out some other way of going about it, that's all. We'll have to drop the idea of establishing a series of camps up the Face, owing to prevailing conditions that look impossible. We'll have to try for the summit carrying everything with us—tents, cooker, sleeping-bags, the lot. Don't you agree, chaps?"

Unanimous approval.

"Looked at like that," said Réné, "I couldn't agree more. But there must be a Camp II; after that we'll see."

"Pooh," laughed Edmond, "it's a piece of cake. Next time it's in the bag!"

The council of war finished on this optimistic note, and we all went outside and enjoyed a magnificent sunset. The sky above us, like an immense vellum, was tinted with all shades of blue, from pale azure to deep lilac. The mountain crests were a flaming orange and the upper part of the Face sparkled, transforming the séracs into scintillating pinnacles of topaz, stand-out from the velvet blue of the sky.

Adrien got extremely busy taking colour photos. Gradually this gorgeous spectacle decreased in splendour, the colours became less vivid and then the sun disappeared altogether. Immediately the sky changed like litmus paper, the walls assumed a livid hue and the hanging glaciers hovered like violet monsters. Only the lower band of séracs still caught the last fleeting rays of the sun and shone like a lighthouse suspended in mid-air.

As we were turning in, a bitter wind suddenly shook the tents, but the sky was clear and it was very cold. Lucien tapped me on the shoulder.

"That wind doesn't mean a thing; it's simply a 'clearing-up wind', which will be followed by fine weather."

I agreed:

"Yes, that's it, just like Chamonix, I think the snow is low enough now and this cold means a really fine spell."

We were not wrong, for next day there was a clear blue sky without the slightest trace of cloud. During the morning we got ready to go up once again to Camp I. The Face was not in ideal condition, but we couldn't wait any longer; we just had to get going—a natural reaction after the enforced leisure of the past few days. The party consisted of Robert, Adrien, Pierre and myself. Lucien decided to stay behind to allow his cut to heal, and Edmond was suffering from blisters on his heels.

We took with us 260 feet of Army hemp rope to replace the fixed nylon rope on the Face. We felt that we should need all the best equipment for the final assault, so we proposed to get together as much nylon rope as possible, as it was much lighter and stronger and also easier to handle when cold. We left Base Camp at 5 p.m. and reached Camp I at half-past six, thereby establishing a new record.

The snow had melted and the camp looked as usual. The tents had stood up magnificently, and the insides of the sleeping-bags were quite dry, the only casualties being some slabs of chocolate and packets of cigarettes affected by moisture. Our anxieties were thus instantly removed and we did our usual jobs with pleasure; even the task of collecting water from the couloir passed off without incident.

Contrary to what we had expected, it was not at all cold; in view of the snowfall, we had thought that the temperature would have been much lower, and were agreeably surprised. The state of the Spur looked favourable, and we went to bed full of optimism for the morning.

I shared the 'isothermic' tent with Adrien, and when we were comfortably settled in our sleeping-bags, I said:

"Didi, what about a last cigarette?"

"Yes, rather."

Using a meat tin as an ashtray, we parted the tent-flaps and lit up. We smoked in silence for a while, enjoying it to the full.

"Do you remember the good old times? . . . It takes us back a bit, doesn't it? How long have we known each other? About ten years, isn't it?"

"More than that—twelve at the least."

"It's funny to meet again on the South Face of Aconcagua!"

"Yes, if anyone had told me that only a year ago, I'd have just laughed at them."

There was silence for a while: we were absorbed in our memories.

"What are our chances tomorrow?"

"Oh, we'll make it all right. Even if there's a lot of snow, we can manage, now that we've got the fixed ropes."

"Yes, surely; and we've just got to find a site for this blessed Camp II."

Our cigarettes were finished, and this terminated the conversation. We were sorely tempted to light up again, but we had to be sensible and think of the morrow.

We were awakened from sleep by a din like the end of the world, and the tent shook like a leaf. An avalanche! This time we've had it! A cloud of powdered snow swept in through the tent door, smothering us in its cold embrace. The rumbling died away, all was quiet once more and we could see the sky again. We heard Robert exclaiming from the other tent:

"Phew, that was a near one! We're full of snow here."

"So are we. It must have gone down the couloir. It's lucky we weren't fetching water. It's the first time we've had a big one like that."

"It's not surprising, with all this new snow."

"Let's hope it's finished, because frankly it's not so funny!"

We lay down again, but couldn't sleep.

We left camp next morning at a quarter past eight with heavy loads. We were carrying the hemp ropes as replacement for those of nylon, all the extra supplies for the elusive Camp II and two light tents for the attack on the summit.

We met the first snow at the foot of the fixed ropes. "Robert's pitch", which lay in the shade, was transformed into a snow wall, all the holds were covered with a layer of floury snow, which stuck to our Vibram soles, making them very slippery. We were forced to pull up on the ropes, which was hard work with our heavy sacks, and by the time we had reached the top of the pitch we were all in.

Fortunately, the "grey couloirs", being well exposed to the sun, were free of snow. Higher up, in the region of the Towers, the terrain was too steep to retain much snow, and we had no trouble at all, but we were very glad that we had equipped them with ropes before the onset of the bad weather, for in their present state they would have been quite impassable without them.

As we went up we exchanged the nylon for the hemp ropes. We stopped at our supply dump, and then went on, bending under the heavy sacks, weighing more than 40 lb. We got to the foot of the Great Towers at half-past one. It was out of the question to ascend the following pitches with such a load, so we had to improvise. Having attached the sacks to a piton, Robert climbed up to an intermediate stance, bringing up Adrien after him. They then threw a rope down, to which Pierre and I attached the first sack. This lifting device was completed by an extra rope which we paid out as our friends hauled up the load. This enabled us to control the ascent of the sack and pull back the "hauling" rope for another load as soon as the operation was completed.

Everything went according to plan, except that our human winches complained of cramp in their arms. Pierre and I had little to do but exhort them to even greater efforts! To the accompaniment of cries and oaths, the four sacks were hauled up to the stance. Robert thereupon climbed the second crack leading to the top of the Towers.

When he got there, a rather difficult conversation ensued. Adrien could not see Robert, and found difficulty in hearing him, owing to the echo from the chimney.

"Adrien . . . you must come up . . . to hoist the sacks again . . . but first of all bring up Guy . . . to the stance . . . with some rope."

"O.K.; come on, Guy!"

It was now my turn. Having tied a 200-foot rope round my shoulders I started up the pitch, dragging behind me the rope connecting me with Pierre. Adrien kept the rope taut and I gave full marks to the leader of this difficult pitch—in fact I was very glad to be belayed from above, and made full use of the fixed étriers. The perpendicular chimney terminated in an overhang thickly coated with ice, and the sight of the last few feet filled me with respectful admiration for Robert. Panting for breath, I asked myself the inevitable question of the second man on the rope: "If you'd had to lead that, what would you have done?"

As I could not find a suitable answer, I sank my pride and asked Adrien: "Can I take a pull on the rope?"

"Yes, come on; I'm well placed."

I left the last piton and, after a struggle, aided by a good pull on the rope, I reached the small stance.

I got my breath back while Adrien took my rope off

the belay, and looked down to the valley. The narrow ledge in the middle of the Face on which we stood was extremely airy and exposed. The drop below us was positively terrifying, so that I instinctively recoiled and cast an anxious glance at the two pitons which alone held us and our sacks. Immediately below us—100 feet lower down—the bronzed face of Pierre could just be seen, conspicuous against the grey of the rocks. Below, the Little Towers, the grey couloirs flecked with snow, down the centre of which ran the ribbon of our fixed ropes, swept downwards in a succession of tremendous leaps, looking like an immense toboggan run. Owing to the perspective, we could not follow them throughout their entire length, neither could we see all the Spur, which reappeared far below, resembling the prow of a ship as it plunged down to the glacier. Still further away, almost hidden in the brown of the moraine, we could just distinguish the tents of Base Camp.

Adrien left the stance and disappeared in the top chimney, while I unravelled the ropes, which had got into a tangle as a result of the complicated manœuvres, and brought up Pierre.

"What a ruddy awful pitch!" said he as he stood beside me; "and not too much room here either."

We could scarcely move, standing in a jumble of ropes which looked as though they could never be separated again. Our four large sacks reduced still more the very limited space at our disposal, leaving hardly any room for the very tricky job of "hauling".

Robert shouted down to us: "I'm ready; send up the first sack." The drag of the rope loosened stones, which richocheted down the chimney and fell on us. It was impossible to get out of their way, and we had to submit to the bombardment for a couple of hours, clinging to our precarious stance.

At last everything was hauled up to the top of the Towers, but we still had not solved the important problem of Camp II. We had hoped to have the time to go up higher in search of a site, but it was already half-past six, and unless we were going to bivouac, we would have to think about going down again.

Adrien and Robert tied the sacks to a rope sling while Pierre and I began to descend the face of the Towers, unbelayed. Once we had reached the couloirs we were on familiar ground, and our slide down the fixed ropes must have broken all speed records. It was no longer just a descent, but rather a sort of controlled fall. Gone was the apprehension of the first few days, and we fairly leaped down the ropes, which we had previously treated with such respect.

We occasionally stopped at one or other of the stances to recover our breath, and while doing so arrived at a definite conclusion: this was the last time we would turn back; we had had more than enough. We would ascend once more, and, this time, would go on to the summit.

When I reached the terrace of the camp, Lucien and Edmond were already there preparing their evening meal. We exchanged the usual pleasantries and then became aware that there was something unusual about their attitude. They were both freshly shaved, with clean shirts, and Lucien offered me a glass of wine from their bottle. While I drank it I noticed that he was watching me. There was something going on—something decidedly fishy. My gaze happened to fall on their sacks, and I saw that they had got out their high-altitude clothing, gloves, etc., and I began to gain an inkling of what it all meant.

"You're not by any chance thinking of starting a rival expedition?"

"Well—er, yes, more or less. . . ."

"You know there is nothing much doing above the Towers."

"Maybe, maybe not. . . ."

Lucien plunged in:

"Now look. It's quite simple. We shan't come down again: we shall go right on to the top."

This rather unexpected decision called forth a chorus of exclamations and questions.

"But Camp II isn't there yet!"

"That doesn't matter; we'll establish it tomorrow and then go on next day."

"What does Réné say to all this?"

"He agrees that we should have a crack."

We were rather disappointed at the idea of this new plan, for we thought that they would establish Camp II the next day and would then come down again to Base Camp so we could start out all together for the final assault on the summit.

In face of their determination, Robert rebelled and protested. He wanted to go along with them, stay up there, and continue on up the next day. It took us ten minutes to induce him to change his mind. We had done enough for one day, and if we wished to make a final assault, we must make the most of our chances. Therefore it was reasonable to go down again, and rest for a couple of nights and a day before starting off once more. Further, we had to assemble equipment and food. All this finally convinced Robert, and although a little upset, we set off for Base Camp, after having wished Lucien and Edmond every success in their venture.

It was completely dark by the time we reached Base Camp, after stumbling about for some time among the stones of the moraine. They had waited dinner for us. Having drunk a good number of glasses of tomato juice, we sat down to our meal. At last we felt completely relaxed and went early to bed.

Chapter Three

COMBINED ATTACK

THE morning of February 18th passed peacefully. We spent some time observing the Face through our glasses, and what we saw confirmed our predictions.

Lucien and Edmond had left Camp I early. Travelling light, they made rapid progress, and reached the top of the Great Towers in an hour and a half, easily beating all speed records. We left our observation post and went and had our lunch. Nothing was likely to happen on the Spur for at least an hour or two, for they were on the normal route.

The meal developed into an animated discussion, everyone aired his views; one thing, however, was certain: tomorrow, come what may, we would start in pursuit of the others.

"You know, I don't like the idea of those two being alone up there," said Robert. "It's not quite right."

"Nonsense, Robert," cut in Réné; "it's quite normal. I know very well that you did all you could to rope the Spur, but I let them go because I judged the moment had arrived. I didn't want them to lose two days waiting about. Even if it isn't so nice, you have to sacrifice yourself, if necessary, for the success of the whole party."

"I know, I know," grumbled Robert; "but all the same. . . ."

"Don't worry," said Adrien, with a smile; "we'll catch them up all right."

"Even if they don't wait for us now," said Pierre, "my

128

opinion is that they'll wait for us at Camp II, and then we'll all go on together."

We had been talking about this hypothetical camp for so long that we thought it about time to look and see whether our friends had actually succeeded in finding a site for it. We sent Robert outside to have a look, and he came back after a few minutes saying that he thought he saw a blue tent about 150 feet above the top of the Towers, just at the foot of the Middle Glacier. Everybody rushed outside to the telescopes. We could see two silhouettes gyrating round a geometrical shape faintly visible against the background of grey rock. After a lively argument, in which Antinucci, Ramazzi and the soldiers took part, we arrived at the conclusion that Camp II had been established at last.

This feat was celebrated by the firing of several pistol shots, which we fondly hoped would be heard by our friends up aloft. During the afternoon we looked out our snow-gaiters, which we had not used up to now, in order to adjust them to our boots.

One would have imagined that there was nothing simpler than to fix them, especially as the obliging manufacturers had kindly provided instructions for fixing them. Having read these instructions we soon realised that we could not understand a word of them, and a glance at the faces of our friends confirmed our suspicions that they were in the same predicament. Nothing happened as it should according to the detailed drawings: either the supports bent, or they jumped out of the holder provided and got lost in the stones. So when night fell we abandoned the unequal struggle and left the gaiters severely alone.

By half-past nine we were all assembled in the great mess-tent. The traditional chicken soup was steaming in the duralumin plates, and the torch, perched on a jam tin, spread a warm and comforting light over the proceedings. Our table, made of planks from the new refuge, gave off a slight smell of resin, and the leather bags serving as chairs reflected the soft light from their polished surfaces. To one side the cooker sang, keeping the sausages-and-mash hot. A real Base Camp atmosphere! An armistice had been declared, we were far from the mountain, and once we had let down the tent-flaps we forgot the very existence of the Face. We had often sat round this table during the last few weeks. Like peasants in the communal farm kitchen, we had the feeling of fatigue in the small of the back common to those who work on the land, and the same feeling of well-being after a hard day's work.

The worries and dangers of the morrow did not concern us—it was our friends' turn. We had supplied the tools for the job, it was up to them, and we followed their efforts with tranquillity—indeed, almost with detachment.

We had well earned a couple of days' rest and two good nights; all we asked for was that these days should be a complete contrast from those spent on the mountain.

We had not yet really come to grips with the heart of the problem; we were not yet fully committed, and had only established advanced posts made possible by the use of the fixed ropes.

In fact, the atmosphere of this meal was rather like that of vigil before a battle. We were preparing to cut loose from Base Camp, having made our decision to "come out at the top".

Contrary to our usual custom, the tent door was wide open. Framed in this triangle of night, the Face rose straight up before us, its great barrier of rock and ice illuminated by the pale light of the moon. For the first time some of us were spending the night at over 16,000 feet, alone amid the stupendous chaos. We ate in silence, awaiting their signals. I looked at my watch for the umpteenth time. Twenty minutes to ten. It could not be long now. I was sitting close to the door, and kept a sharp look-out on the dark mountain.

Suddenly I perceived a faint gleam. I was immediately struck by the impression of distance compared with the signals we used to receive from Camp I; the comparative feebleness of the glimmer made it seem all the further off, and the darkness of the night, which did not permit us to see the full extent of the Spur, only accentuated the distance, and made it look like the mast-light of a great ocean liner. We all rushed outside, waving our electric torches. Robert had picked up the large hurricane lamp, and brandished it at arm's length. With his hat, he looked rather like a station-master giving the right-away to an important train. Away up the Face a much brighter light appeared, which gradually increased in intensity.

"Bengal lights!"

"It's green!"

"Terrific! Surely they'll let off another one!"

This running commentary was carried on at great speed, as though we were trying to say everything before the light was extinguished. Madame Antinucci was in raptures at this curious display of fireworks taking place in the middle of the South Face, but fully realised never-theless, the significance for us of this simple green flame.

The light slowly died away, leaving only a small red spot which burned up suddenly and then blacked out. We waited in vain for a second signal. We must reply to them before they went into their tent for the night.

"Find a green flare," said Réné to Pierre, who was rummaging in the store tent; "we must reply with the same colour."

"I can't find the damn things!"

"They're there all right, down by the sardines, on top of the boxes of nougat."

The flame stabbed the darkness, lighting us all up and casting grotesque shadows on the tents and rocks. The light died away, and we stared fixedly at the dark Face, but there was no answering signal. It was very cold, so we slowly went back into the tent and closed the flap behind us. There were now two distinct parties, one below and one above.

Réné was still in pain from his bad leg. He was not able to sit still for any length of time, and went to bed immediately. As it was still quite early, and we were not sleepy, we turned the tent once more into a games-room. The Doctor and Pierre started a game of chess, watched by Robert and Adrien. Madame Antinucci and Suzanne played canasta against Ramazzi and me.

Engrossed in the cards or chess game, we hoped for the time being to forget tomorrow.

A knave—I was glad it did not take the kitty! Check to the king. Pierre was just gaining time in order not to think of what might await us up there. How will we react above 20,000 feet? The Rock Wall. . . . How long will it take to climb? Suppose we can't get through the séracs?

"Guy, you're asleep; it's your turn to play!"

"Eh. . . . Oh sorry! There, ten of clubs."

Suzanne raked in a huge kitty. I saw a faint sign of annoyance flit over my partner's face, apparently my mind was not on the game. Alongside me it was the same.

"My dear Pierre check and mate!"

The Doctor had won. We went back to our tents, but before we turned in we smoked a last cigarette, still thinking about the others. . . . What were Lucien and Edmond going to do tomorrow? Go on or wait for us? As I returned to my tent I stole a glance at the Face, and immediately fell over a guy-rope—they always seemed to be in the way, somehow.

Réné could not sleep.

"Guy, give me an injection; otherwise I'll keep you awake all night."

THE ONLY TENT OF CAMP II WAS ERECTED ON A NARROW LEDGE

EDMOND DENIS AND GUY POULET ASCEND THE MIDDLE GLACIER, 18,370′

I went outside to sterilise the syringe, and this time succeeded in avoiding the guy-ropes.

Robert and Adrien were still in the mess-tent.

"It's a funny thing," said Adrien, "that they didn't let off a red flare after the green one, to show that they were going on tomorrow. It puzzles me."

"I know," said Robert. "I think there's no doubt that they aren't going to. I know Lucien; they'll do their level best to stay where they are and not come down. Don't you agree, Guy?"

"I'll tell you what I think. They may have got a bit above themselves, but they're not mad. They've got to bear in mind first of all that the last 6,000 feet would be a bit sticky for a rope of two, and furthermore that they haven't got enough food to go on. That alone decides it, as I see it."

Robert was not quite satisfied, but Adrien saw my point and agreed.

It was half-past twelve. Robert remarked that it was already tomorrow and high time we were in bed. After I had injected Réné, I got into my sleeping-bag and, contrary to my expectations, went to sleep almost at once.

February 19th, 8.30 a.m.

The sun was already shining on the tent. Without getting out of my sleeping-bag, I picked up my glasses and focused them on the top of the Towers. I found the tent, but could see no trace of our friends. I searched slowly across the Middle Glacier . . . nothing to be seen. Robert appeared; he had just been looking through the telescope.

"Well?"

"What, you haven't seen them? They've already got as far as the Rock Wall!"

I leapt out of my sack and frantically searched the cliff from top to bottom.

"I can't find them. Where did you pick them up?"

"Ha, ha," laughed Robert. "Ever been had? I just pulled your leg. I've been looking for them since seven o'clock."

"It's not funny. At the same time I'm rather surprised; and, on the other hand, it's extraordinary if they haven't started."

We all took turns at the telescope while preparing breakfast. Suddenly, about ten o'clock, Pierre shouted, "I've found them!"

There they were—two little figures, one blue and one red—outside the tent. A quarter of an hour later they began to ascend slowly among the grey rocks immediately above Camp II. We were astonished at this late start, as we expected that they would have got away early in order to get as high as possible in the course of the day.

The time of waiting and uncertainty was over, we had only to follow the course of events, and we experienced a feeling of relief. We began to get ready to start, and at last got the snow gaiters fixed in position, and while my friends were sorting everything out, I assembled the first-aid kit.

We were going to take some energy pills with us * which we hoped would decrease our breathlessness and fatigue. We had tried them out while we were fixing the ropes on the Spur, and had found them quite satisfactory.

I encountered some difficulty in inducing my friends, who were not drug-minded, to take the various vitamin preparations recommended to me by several doctors who had acted as medical advisers to the expedition. I found that considerable eloquence and not a little psychology were necessary to get them accepted, with the notable exception of Pierre, who was always ready to try anything new, especially if it had a sweet taste!

Dr. Antinucci advised me to increase the amount of coramin. In case of cardiac-pulmonary exhaustion, I

* These pills consisted mainly of adenosin-5-tri-phosphoric acid, generally known as A.T.P.

took along two flasks of this preparation in a drinkable form, as well as phials for injection. While all these preparations were being made, our friends had reached the Middle Glacier and were ascending it very slowly. From their slow gait we assumed that the snow was most likely deep and probably treacherous; they had to consolidate their steps and made frequent halts.

Robert called me over to check the stores and equipment. Spread out on the ground, it presented an imposing collection. Robert and Pierre had arranged it under different categories. The food consisted of the following: soup, eight boxes of Ovomaltine, chocolate, nougat, two kinds of sausages, biscuits, cheese, a petrol cooker and about $3\frac{1}{2}$ pints of fuel. In addition to all this everyone was taking along a certain amount of sugar, dried fruit and mint pastilles for thirst. All this was personal equipment and was distributed in our various pockets.

As regards climbing gear, we took along everything we had left: twenty rock and ice pitons and the same number of duralumin karabiner, two axes, two pairs of crampons and a quantity of line for making slings.

We now examined our altitude clothing. We each took with us one pair of thin socks and a pair of woollen stockings with the grease left in, one pair of long pants, climbing trousers made of thick cloth and provided with a nylon snow- and wind-proof covering. On the upper part of the body we wore two shirts, a down waistcoat, a down coat, anorak, scarf and a woollen hat. We also carried a long anorak for bivouac purposes, a nylon quilted sleeping-sack, a spare pair of socks and two or three spare pairs of gloves. In addition to all this, Adrien and I, who were in charge of the photographic equipment, had red silk over-gloves, allowing easy manipulation of the cameras.

Somehow or other we contrived to stow all this in our four sacks, each of which weighed about 30 lb. All that was left were the cameras and films, consisting of a small 16-mm. camera with ten spools, a "Foca" (24 × 36 mm.) holding thirty-six exposures with a spare film—all in colour.

Now at last we were ready.

Lucien and Edmond were making painfully slow progress and had scarcely got half-way up the glacier, which seemed inexplicable to us. Réné was still in pain, and the slightest movement hurt him. Dr. Antinucci tried to ease him by a variety of injections, intravenous and local. It was difficult to say which had the most effect on him: the disease, the treatment or his enforced inactivity.

Madame Antinucci came out to tell us lunch was ready. Although we had not much appetite, we made ourselves eat "to conserve our strength". Conversation languished, we kept going outside to take a look through the telescope.

"What are they doing?"

"Just the same—advancing slowly."

At about 3 p.m. they stopped and sat down on the snow—they were about half-way up the glacier now. They stayed there a long time and then descended in their tracks. We did not know what to make of this retreat. We were almost glad that they were not going on, and at the same time sorry to see them forced to retreat. Once more doubt assailed us, had they found out that the Rock Wall was unclimbable?

We decided to postpone our departure for Camp I, in order to see what they were going to do. While the others had their siesta, we stayed in the mess-tent, chain smoking, and worn out with trying to find the right answer to the conundrum. Somebody suggested making coffee—just for something to do. At half-past four Lucien and Edmond had got back to Camp II. We could see them walking round the tent, but there was no sign of them continuing the descent. They must be waiting for us.

We got dressed and checked over everything for the last time. We were quite ready, but could not make the effort to start, feeling strangely united, apart from the others, in the store tent. We had already ceased to be a part of the camp. Mercedes came to tell us that the mule was ready. Robert waved him away. It was past five. Just a few more minutes—we would really start at a quarter past. We had just time left for another cigarette, and sat down on our baggage, smoking and looking nervously at our watches. We felt like bull-fighters waiting to go into the arena, only our arena was vertical and we would have to fight alone, without the *vivas* of an acclaiming public.

A quarter past five. It was time to go! Réné was standing at the entrance to the tent holding on to the tent-pole. We shook him by the hand and tried to make jokes.

"Well, chaps, don't take too many risks, and see that you do it."

Dr. and Madame Antinucci embraced us with tears in their eyes, and Ramazzi vigorously shook hands. Mercedes had gone ahead with his mule. We looked back for a last farewell. A light breeze stirred the flags; the doctor waved and called out:

"Good luck and *Vive la France.*"

We turned away, to hide our emotion, and followed the mule in the direction of the glacier. Mercedes was waiting for us at the foot of the névé. He had led the mule rather further than usual, but now it refused to go on. Humping our heavy sacks, we severed the last link with Base Camp and started on the monotonous and laborious trek up the glacier. As we got to the bergschrund we heard shouts from above and looking up saw a figure gesticulating at the top of the Towers, 3,000 feet higher up. In spite of the vast distance, we managed to catch a few words here and there.

"Have . . . you . . . got everything. . . ."

Shouting at the top of our voices, we replied in the affirmative.

"Want . . . pitons . . . equipment. . . ."

Same reply.

The apparition was apparently satisfied, and seized the opportunity of adding a few rude words, to which we replied with some phrases from our very rich vocabulary chosen as being most suitable for transmission at this great distance. Needless to say, this conversation was quite unprintable!

Lucien, for it was he, disappeared from view with a last gesture. We continued on our way, and reached Camp I in less than an hour and a quarter, in spite of the weight of our sacks. We were indisputably in fine fettle, and to judge from our recent conversation, our friends seemed also to be in great form.

After collecting the water, and having partaken of a very light-hearted evening meal, we went to bed without waiting for the signals from Base Camp. When they did come we replied to them from the comfort of our sleeping-bags.

We smoked a last cigarette and talked optimistically of our chances the next day. It was a quiet night, but, as usual, I did not sleep well.

February 20th

We left camp at eight o'clock, after having carefully closed the tents and strengthened the guy-ropes with some rocks, for we did not know how long we should be away. It was cold, and we were very heavily laden. Nevertheless we soon reached the equipment dump, where we picked up an altitude tent and two ice-axes. We had some difficulty in dragging these large sacks up the ropes fixed on the Little Towers, and we did not get to the foot of the Great Towers until just before midday. Lucien and Edmond must have been watching us, for the former suddenly appeared at the top.

"Hullo, boys! How's it going?"

"Very well, thanks. And you?"

"Smashing! Have you brought anything to eat?"

There was no doubt that they had thought of nothing else since yesterday.

"Yes, we've got everything."

"Fine! Pitons and karabiner too?"

"Yes; don't worry."

"O.K. Do you want us to help you with your sacks?"

We all answered together, like school-boys who had been promised a holiday: "Oh yes, please!"

We thought it advisable to add a few flattering words so that they would not go back on their offer. We got to work on the job of hoisting up the sacks, and decided to do without the half-way stance and hoist direct with a single 260-foot span. Lucien threw down the 230-foot nylon rope, to which we tied on another of 200 feet and 130 feet of line. When everything was ready, Pierre and I attached the first sack and told Lucien to haul it up.

"It's mine," said Pierre. "See what he says when he starts pulling it up. He's going to have a surprise."

The rope tightened and the sack began to rise slowly up the rocks, and then swung out below the great overhang at the top of which stood Lucien. We guided its progress and paid out the rope when necessary, but could not prevent the friction of the rope on the rocks from sending stones down on top of us.

"It's going all right," said Pierre. "Fortunately we're used to it by now."

With a grating noise of steel on rock, the sack swung over the crest and disappeared from view. It had panned out just right: we had only a few feet of slack left.

Lucien reappeared: "What on earth have you got in that sack; it weighs a ton?"

"We know," said Pierre. "We've had them on our backs all morning. You can't tell us anything!"

Adrien filmed the hoisting of the three remaining

sacks. Cutting out the stance saved time. Nevertheless it took us more than an hour and a half to get them all up.

Having thus got rid of our burdens, we started up the pitch. After the stance came a deep chimney, much less exposed than the first one, but obstructed by projecting rocks and full of ice. By dint of much wedging and wriggling I reached the exit of the crack though in an exhausted condition. When Pierre joined me he expressed surprise at the terrain ahead of us. We were on a sort of rounded and exposed bastion; 20 feet below was the start of a couloir, from which we were separated by a vertical wall leading up to the Middle Glacier, which was quite close. This couloir was enclosed by very steep and loose rock walls. Somewhat dismayed, we looked for Camp II and, not seeing it, we hailed our friends, who replied from somewhere out of sight. Suddenly Edmond's head appeared from behind a rock about 150 feet above us.

"Here we are!"

"Where's the camp?"

"Just here; but you can't see the tent from below."

We climbed down the wall and got into the couloir. When we had ascended about a rope's length we found a second couloir, previously hidden from sight by a bulge in the face. It was very steep, abounding in huge icicles and terminated in a narrow chimney. A final pull up and I was out, when, to my surprise, I saw the one tent comprising Camp II just in front of me. I took off my sack and looked around.

The tent was balanced on a sort of rock hog's back formed by the junction of several couloirs which plunged down on either side towards the Great Towers, or terminating above the precipices of the great Central Couloir. It was like being situated at the end of a half-open fan. The guy-ropes of the ridge-pole were attached to pitons, while those on the side facing the valley hung down loose, weighted with large stones. The Face con-

tinued upwards in a succession of slabs as far as the
Middle Glacier, which ascended with a uniform surface
as far as the Rock Wall. As seen from here, it looked quite
unclimbable—a compact mass of brown rocks in which
the eye vainly endeavoured to find any means of progress
up the smooth 250-foot wall.

The top was surmounted by a sort of crown formed by
the crystal-clear pinnacles of the séracs of the Upper
Glacier, parts of which were overhanging and in a state
of dubious equilibrium.

Pierre, Robert and Adrien now emerged from the
chimney, and each in turn glanced quickly at the tent
and then upwards, taking in all the details of the
stupendous panorama.

The exit from the chimney ushered us into a new
world, the region of high altitudes. The tip of the Spur
stood out as it were beyond a mysterious ceiling, which
had hitherto concealed from us this new and strange
world. The Face had suddenly widened out—the rocks,
the snow and ice, even the light itself, appeared quite
different: purer, more brilliant and indisputably more
hostile.

Lucien and Edmond looked at us in silence. Like old
hands they watched the reactions of the "new boys".
Robert was the first to break the pregnant silence:

"It's amazing! What a change! What's above this?
And why did you come down at three o'clock yesterday?
Come on, tell us all about it!"

They looked at one another, and then Lucien said:

"Well, I'll put it into a few words. We got to the
top of the Great Towers very early the day before yesterday—I expect you saw us through the glasses? Right!
We hauled up the sacks and looked for a site for the tent.
Well, you can see what we found. We were jolly pleased
to be able to put up a tent at all. We started out yesterday morning . . ."

"But why so late?" interposed Pierre.

"Wait till tomorrow and you'll see," smiled Edmond.

"We left carrying a tent, hoping to get somewhere near the summit," continued Lucien. "Suddenly we ran into difficulties"—he pointed to the rocks just above the camp —"rotten rock all the way. We had to fix more than 300 feet of rope before we reached the glacier. When we got there, the snow was up to our thighs and lying on top of ice. It's awful trying to make tracks in that."

"But you started early; the condition of the snow should surely have been good enough," said Adrien.

Edmond shook his head.

"That snow up there never changes—it doesn't get hot enough in the day-time: it was always powder."

Lucien went on:

"When we found that we were making such slow progress, we came to the conclusion that it was impossible for the two of us to go on alone, so we came back."

"And what's more, we'd had nothing to eat," said Edmond peevishly.

I eagerly plied Lucien with questions:

"You got about half-way up the glacier, so you must have had a good view of the Rock Wall. What do you think of it?"

Lucien shrugged his shoulders.

"I think it'll 'go', but we'll have to give it all we've got. By the way, have you brought plenty of pitons?"

"Don't worry," said Robert cheerfully, "keep your hair on. We'll be up that cliff tomorrow, even if we have to do it in artificial the whole way. (*Translator's Note:* Artificial climbing is the technique of the progressive use of a combination of pitons and étriers.)

Our two friends did not seem to share our enthusiasm, but Edmond cheered up considerably when he saw the food which we had turned out of our sacks. Without wasting time he began to melt snow over the little butane-gas-cooker. Meanwhile, Lucien was leaping about outside the tent taking photographs. He jumped with great accuracy from rock to rock, overhanging a drop of some 4,000 feet.

Edmond looked at us and made a face:

"That's been going on for two days. I just can't look at him, it gives me the willies to see him doing it unroped. I'm frightened he'll suddenly disappear."

Lucien made a rude reply and, having taken one photo, rushed off to an even more precarious position to take another.

"Just in case you should suddenly leave us," said Pierre icily, "at least leave the camera behind; it's valuable!"

Adrien also took advantage of the light to film the camp, while Robert, Pierre and I got on with the job of preparing a flat surface where three of us could spend the night. However, in spite of an enormous amount of hard work, we soon realised that it was manifestly impossible to level enough ground to put up another tent. Three of us, therefore, would have to bivouac. Adrien, Pierre and Robert agreed to do this, and I shared the tent with Edmond and Lucien.

Edmond, our cook, told us to come and get our Ovomaltine, which he had just made, and asked for snow to make the soup with.

"I'll go," said Lucien. "I know a place where there are some lovely icicles; you get more water that way."

He moved off a few yards, and suddenly fell up to his shoulders in a crack in the rock, amid much crashing of displaced boulders. One large rock, disturbed by his fall, bounded down the invisible chasm with a sinister, hollow sound. We threw down a rope to help him out, to the accompaniment of suitable jokes.

"He's getting so bored with his friends, he wants to be alone!"

"It was a loose rock which gave under my feet; actually I meant to go down there, but not quite so quickly!"

When he had extricated himself we saw that there was a vertical shaft, through which we could see the foot of the Great Couloir, about 3,000 feet below.

"I should be very glad," said Robert curtly, "if you would kindly stop this fooling around and get the ice from the chimney we came up—and roped, if you don't mind!"

We arranged the bivouac with the help of the two tents we had brought with us, one serving as a ground-sheet, the other providing shelter of a sort.

The sun disappeared suddenly behind the South Arête, and the temperature immediately dropped several degrees. Within half an hour, although the rocks were still warm, the thermometer had fallen to freezing point.

Our gas cylinder was empty and we had to make do with petrol cookers to heat up the soup. The new burners absorbed a lot before they caught alight—we ought, of course, to have brought partly used burners, which would have required less fuel. This apparently insignificant detail assumed considerable importance in the days to come.

In view of the hard work ahead of us, we had a large meal—soup, sausage, cheese, nougat and tinned fruit, washed down with "Tupungato": the local red wine from Mendoza. The cold was piercing, so we did not delay going to bed. After we had tucked Adrien, Pierre and Robert into their bivouac, we tried to arrange ourselves comfortably in our small high-altitude tent. When all was settled, I asked Edmond to make some Ovomaltine.

"A good idea," said he; "it'll take our minds off things until it's time for the signals."

We asked the others how they were settling down, and they replied that they were all right. When the Ovomaltine was ready I took a tinful over to them and found them buried in their sleeping-bags with only their faces showing. Having got ready the Bengal light and placed it within reach just outside the tent door, I hurriedly slid down again between my two companions. Time passed very slowly, we were all smoking, and the tent was soon full of smoke, which wafted outside. At half-past nine Lucien stretched out an arm and lit the flare, as a signal to Réné that we were going on tomorrow. Then we tried to sleep.

Lucien and Edmond were lying with their heads towards the main door, while I was in the middle, facing the opposite way. My door was partially blocked by gravel, and I was half suffocated. After a few minutes pushing with my heels I managed to get the opening clear, and felt better. I couldn't get off to sleep—I was too hot, and each time I began to doze I awoke with a sensation of suffocation and had to stick my head out under the brailing. My friends, on the other hand, complained of cold.

Little by little the pale light of dawn filtered through the walls of the tent. From outside we could hear a few short meaningless phrases like those one hears in a railway compartment very early in the morning when one of the passengers has just pulled up the blind, disclosing a bleak, grey dawn.

At last the tent lit up with the rays of the rising sun and everything was transformed—tomorrow had finally come.

We could hear Robert talking about getting up, but without much conviction. We did not make a move before nine o'clock, and breakfast restored our energy. Robert called out to Lucien:

"Well, have you made up your mind? Are you going down or coming with us? You'd better decide quickly; it's getting late."

"Don't imagine you're going up there alone. Who'd pull you up to the top if I wasn't there!"

"Right," said Robert; "and you, Edmond?"

"Me? Don't single me out: I'm quite happy with you all, and intend to go with you, I should get bored alone."

We had never really thought that they would leave us,

but their jesting put new heart into us. Our morale was high—we were ready to attack. Our faces lit up, and Adrien slapped Lucien vigorously on the back.

We rapidly prepared our sacks, having divided everything into six equal parts in such a way that each of us carried some food and climbing equipment, so that we should not be too badly off if one of the sacks got lost.

Having seen to the tent and tightened the guy-ropes, I had a last look round inside, and noted with regret that we could not take our air mattresses with us. I left some exposed films and a camera, which we would pick up when the camp was evacuated. Everything was ready, and at last we could start. It was a quarter past ten—the same time that Lucien and Edmond had left, so we hadn't got away any earlier after all.

We left camp on three ropes. Lucien and Robert went off first, followed by Pierre and Adrien, who had chosen this position for taking photographs. My rope brought up the rear, with Edmond leading. Sixty feet above the camp we found the two ropes already fixed by our friends two days ago. The first of these we left, but took the second one with us for future use. We had therefore with us, a 230-foot nylon rope, two more of 200 feet (all of 8-mm. diameter), and a 130-foot rope for belaying purposes (6 mm. diameter). In addition, we had 100 feet of line for making slings—in all a total of 860 feet of rope.

After having climbed the steep rocks we came to a sort of rounded crest which marked the start of the Middle Glacier. We stopped here on a dry patch of rock to put on our crampons. A few yards ahead the snow started straight up from the rocks—quite abruptly, as is sometimes the case with hanging glaciers. We had reached an imposing arête, the general shape of which was like that of a long-drawn-out S. It was formed by the junction of two separate snow-slopes comprising the glacier. The Spur doubtless continued underneath the rampart of ice which had taken its shape in a softer form.

146

The first two ropes were already at work on the arête, and Edmond and I soon followed in their tracks. Immediately I set foot on it I was surprised by the steepness of the slope, which from observation through our field-glasses we had estimated as not exceeding 35°. In actual fact it was hardly less than 50° and more than that in certain places. (An ice slope of 50° in the Alps, even at a very low altitude, is considered a difficult obstacle.) It was already one o'clock in the afternoon, the layer of fresh snow on the ice reflected a dazzling light, and in spite of our snow-glasses we were forced to keep our eyes half closed, almost blinded by the glare. We went on slowly, taking advantage of the tracks left by our friends.

The route now left the arête and crossed the centre of a field of nieves penitentes. Edmond stopped, and we filled our flasks from a little stream flowing under a thin coating of clear ice. A few gentle blows of an axe made a small basin, and we were soon able to collect over three pints of water, which we drank greedily in great gulps. The others had now got a good way up the slope, so we hastened to catch up with them.

The snow crust—that bugbear of the alpinist—now became very treacherous, we kept sinking in up to our thighs and the effort to withdraw our legs fatigued us greatly. For more than an hour we ploughed our way up this infernal slope. When we finally regained the crest of the arête, the snow cover was thinner, and we were able to adopt a more regular rhythm. In places the slope steepened and ice appeared under the thin cover of floury snow. It was occasionally necessary to cut steps in order to ascend a particularly steep place.

The slope ended abruptly against the rock cliff. There was no bergschrund, but the snow protruded, forming a sort of narrow ledge. Our friends were waiting for us on this cornice. It was 4 p.m. and 18,370 feet. We had reached the foot of the second great obstacle on the Face.

The prospects did not look encouraging. Above us the

smooth and overhanging slabs were quite unclimbable. The sole possibility lay in a chimney about 100 feet to our left, but we were unable to see its exit. However, the quality of the rock had changed, and now seemed much sounder.

"It looks as though we'd got to the foot of the Wall," said Edmond facetiously.

"Well, boys," I said, "what do we do? The chimney, I suppose."

Robert turned and said sarcastically:

"But, my dear chap, what an eye like a hawk you've got! What a route-finder! One of the old school!"

"Joking apart, what are we going to do?"

"This is what I suggest," said Lucien. "We'll have to have a look at this chimney, but we needn't all go. I'll go off on a recce with Robert, and in the meantime you can make a platform—at all costs."

This was agreed to. While they were getting ready, we piled the sacks in a hole in the rocks and set to work on the snow-ledge with our axes. Unfortunately the snow soon gave place to ice, which made our work much more difficult.

Lucien succeeded in getting into the chimney, but could not climb it direct; he hammered in a piton and descended a few feet.

"No go! it's overhanging and the bottom is plastered with ice. I'm going to try the arête."

We all stopped working and watched Lucien spread-eagled on the left wall of the chimney.

"Lulu, there's a hold for your left hand—higher up— just a little further on. . . ."

Balancing carefully on small footholds, he pulled himself up with a great effort, and got on to the arête. We watched in silence, not daring to question him. He turned round and said briefly:

"I'm going on; I think there might be a stance higher up."

AT THE FOOT OF THE 85′ COULOIR IN THE ROCK WALL

GUY POULET AND LUCIEN BERARDINI AT CAMP III, 18,860′

He disappeared behind a bulge in the rock. Minutes passed, and then we heard hammer-blows.

"Robert, you can come."

Much relieved, we went on with our work. We had hoped to be able to put up our tents, but had to give up the idea. It would have taken at least five hours' work to cut a platform large enough in the ice. There was nothing for it but to bivouac. It took two hours' hard work before we had broken up the blocks of ice and swept away enough snow to make sufficient space for six men.

Some icicles fell down the chimney, announcing the return of our two friends. Robert and Lucien soon joined us, having descended the chimney *en rappel*. They made a diagonal rappel (pendule) across the ice slope which separated them from the terrace where we were.

"Well, what does it look like?"

"It's a real swine—steep slabs covered with verglas."

"All the same, it isn't as difficult as the Towers, is it? The rock looked better."

"Pooh! you say it looks better! It's so firm that you can't put in pitons, because all the cracks are bunged up! And there are more than 600 feet like that!"

"At any rate, you think it'll go?" said Pierre. "How far did you get?"

"Oh, two run-outs. We left ropes for tomorrow."

I was absorbing all this. The pitches ahead would no doubt be very difficult, but one sentence of Lucien's was significant; they had fixed ropes, therefore we would go on tomorrow.

Although it was only half-past six, we got our bivouac ready, in order to escape the intense cold. Using the tents as ground-sheets, we crept into our sleeping-bags, all bunched up together. Robert was on cookhouse fatigue. Lying alongside him, I pulled his leg:

"Really, that's not very clever! Surely you should erect a little wall for the cooker, like Camp I . . . remember?"

L   149

"It wouldn't be a bad idea at that! You can laugh if you like, but that won't stop the fuel burning away like nobody's business. I've filled the cooker twice just to boil three pints of water!"

Under prevailing conditions, these cookers used an incredible amount of fuel. They were standing on snow, which, helped by the wind, caused great loss of heat. What was more, petrol evaporates more rapidly at high altitudes, and we had to melt snow to get our water. A tinful of snow produced only a minute quantity of water, and there were six of us.

At the end of an hour, Robert had managed to make some soup and a tinful of Ovomaltine. This, with dried fruit and nougat, completed our meal.

It was much too early to sleep, so we smoked and had a sing-song. In response to a general request, I had to do my famous imitation of Maurice Chevalier, and sang *"Ca s'est passé un dimanche"* (It took place one Sunday). This immediately reminded me of a bivouac with Jacques Poincenot, Réné Ferlet and Maurice Herzog, fastened to pitons on the North Face of Piz Badile. We had practically no food, and about five o'clock in the morning Maurice gave me a bar of chocolate in exchange for a rendering of *"Pecheurs de Perles"* (The Pearl-fishers).

This reminiscence launched us off into opera, and soon the mountains were echoing fragments of *Bohême*, *Carmen* and *Tosca*, Bizet and Puccini must have turned in their graves—unless they were smiling!

Soon it began to get dark, and at half-past nine the lights went on at Base Camp. We lit our red flare—all's well, we're going on. Conversation languished, a rustle of nylon—somebody turning over in his sleeping-bag—then silence. Night took charge, and everyone was left to his own thoughts.

The sun woke us up at half-past six next morning. Adrien knelt up and filmed our awakening and preparations for departure. Pierre had decided to lead, and made up the first rope with Robert. Their job was to find the route and equip the pitches with fixed ropes where necessary, while the other two ropes would follow on, ready to take over when required.

"Just think," said Lucien dolefully; "all that levelling work for only one night!"

"I sincerely hope," said I, "that this evening we shall find somewhere to put up our tents. Personally, I'm not all that keen on bivouacs, especially at this height."

"Let's hope so. Considering what we've been up against up to now, it's about time we had a break!"

"I think we will; it can't go on for ever like this."

The voice of Edmond interrupted our conversation:

"You down there! You can come up now."

Putting on my sack, I took hold of the rope and crossed the ice-slope to get to the foot of the chimney. Last evening Lucien had climbed this pitch by the arête, but today the rope was hanging down the chimney, thus eliminating a dangerous pendulum movement.

I noted the ice-bulge 30 feet higher up, which did not look too pleasant. We were climbing unroped in order to spare as much rope as possible for equipping the mountain. Bracing my feet against the rock, I pulled myself up with some difficulty. The heavy sack was weighing me down, and I reached the base of the overhang quite out of breath. I began to feel signs of cramp in my hand and had some difficulty in hanging on to the rope. I took one glance down towards the glacier far below the base of the chimney. If I slipped, I'd had it! To stop my mounting panic, I employed rush tactics and surmounted the overhang in a desperate effort. I wedged myself in the chimney and, making a hasty loop in the rope, fastened myself to it by means of a karabiner attached to my safety belt. These last three minutes of intense effort had exhausted me for the time being.

A few yards above me, Edmond was sitting in the sun

and watching me in silence. I was still separated from the stance by another ice overhang.

"Is it as bad as the one below?"

"No, it's much less hard on the arms."

"Thank God for that! All the same, I'd be glad if you'd chuck down a rope for the end bit . . . if you can."

"O.K."

Thus belayed, I soon reached the stance. This merely consisted of a single step on a small ridge which petered out against a vertical wall. A rope obliquely mounting a steep slab showed the route followed by the others; it disappeared from view 30 feet away behind a large rock. We could hear some hammering in the distance and then Adrien's voice:

"Come on, Edmond!"

He disappeared from sight at the top of the slab, and I brought Lucien up to me. Attached to a piton, we tried in vain to find a comfortable position. Fortunately we were in the sun and it was not too cold. We had recovered the rope from the chimney, and roped up with it. Time dragged slowly on, and the inactivity and uncertainty began to get us down, when suddenly a yell from above told me to start.

I quickly crossed the slab, and when I got to the other side the rest of the way was open before me.

Enormous slabs of brown rock were superimposed on each other like the tiles on a roof. They were extremely steep, cut across by vertical steps shining with verglas, and terminated 150 feet higher up at the foot of a perpendicular wall from which depended huge cascades of ice.

When I reached the stance, I realised that Pierre had led this 130-foot pitch without even a piton to belay him!

The ensuing run-outs were equally exposed; now and again a piton inserted upside down afforded some slight moral support!

At four o'clock we were once more reunited at the foot

of the Wall. Perhaps reunited is hardly the right way to describe our position, for we were spread out over the slope on small islands of rock emerging from the steep snow-field. Away to our left the séracs of the Upper Glacier could be seen on the skyline, but we were separated from them by this fresh obstacle.

It was about 30 feet high and appallingly steep. The only possibility of scaling it was by an icy chimney about 100 feet to our left. Edmond took over the lead and, wearing crampons, he began a very delicate traverse across ice-coated slabs. Using his marteau-piolet, he nicked tiny hand-holds, the points of his crampons grating on black ice. A short broche was driven with a hollow sound. Infinitely slowly, yard by yard, he crossed the slabs and reached the line of the chimney. Here he hammered in another piton—this time with a clear, ringing note—and attached an étrier, through which he thrust a leg and sat down facing the wall, with his arms hanging down.

Lucien got impatient:

"You're taking a hell of a while. Do you know what time it is? What's he waiting for? Get a move on, Edmond!"

Edmond turned round:

"Have a heart! Let me get my breath! Besides, someone'll have to take over: I just can't climb this ruddy chimney with these blasted spikes on my feet."

"O.K., come on back," said Adrien. "Let me have a crack."

"Listen, Didi," said Robert aggressively. "There's no question of 'having a crack'. You've either got to do it or leave it to us. There's no time to spare."

Adrien looked at him and replied quietly:

"Keep your wool on. I know I said I'd 'have a crack', but I'd do all I could—you know that."

Robert slapped him on the back:

"I'm sorry, old boy. I lost my temper, and didn't

153

mean to hurt your feelings. Carry on; you'll get up all right!"

Edmond made a diagonal rappel back to the stance and Adrien set off for the chimney. By dint of much back- and knee-work he managed to make some progress amid encouragement from the rest of us.

"Nice work, Didi! You've made it! A few more feet and you're up."

After half an hour's exhausting work, the chimney was climbed. While we were hauling up the sacks, Pierre took over the lead and attacked the next pitch. If we should be overtaken by darkness before we could reach the base of the séracs, we would have to spend the night tied on to pitons. We could not see Pierre, but the rope moved up very quickly until there were only a few feet left.

"Pierrot, the rope's nearly out!"

"How much more?"

"Nine or ten feet, not more. Can you see the séracs?"

"Yes, I've just reached the snow; I want my crampons."

"Right-o; Lucien's coming up."

Half an hour passed—it seemed an age. When it came to my turn, the stars were beginning to appear. It was going to be a fight against the dark. I ascended the almost perpendicular ridge at top speed—which Lucien had climbed in a single run-out without pitons. There was no proper belay—the rope was just passed round a slanting spike of rock. Lucien was already 30 feet above, cutting steps up the ice, and after an oblique traverse to the right he disappeared behind a sérac. The slope was evidently less steep, for the rope moved up rapidly. Next moment he called out:

"It's all right, you chaps, we can bivouac among the séracs about 150 feet higher up."

I passed this news down the line. It was quite an acrobatic feat putting on my crampons, as I had to

balance on a rock with one hand on Pierre's head while
trying to fasten the frozen straps with the other. At last I
was ready, and started up the ice slope after Lucien,
while Pierre waited at the belay for his sack to be sent up
by Robert.

Night fell with startling suddenness. I joined Pierre at
the foot of a huge sérac, where the dark forms of our
friends could be seen against the whiteness of the snow.
Tired out to the point of exhaustion we began to dig
away the new snow to make a level platform. Pierre now
arrived, followed by Adrien, and together we set to work
with our axes on the sérac.

All at once a pale light became visible far below on the
glacier; in the excitement of the moment we had completely forgotten the exchange of signals with Base Camp.
A swift blow of an axe and a niche was cut in the ice,
in which we set the flare and ignited it. The red glow
turned the snow a blood-red colour.

"Red! All's well; they're going on", is what they must
have been thinking down there.

All's well! Was it? We were utterly played out and
the biting cold numbed our hands and feet. Darkness had
fallen only half an hour ago, and the temperature was
already down to 10° F.

We spread the two tents on the barely levelled snow
with all possible speed, took off our boots, put them in
our sacks and slipped into our sleeping-bags, huddled
together for warmth.

Gradually we ceased to shiver and circulation was
restored in our frozen hands: we were at last able to
abandon our fight for existence and relax a little.

We had climbed for thirteen hours today without a
drink of any sort, and had only been able to nibble a little
nougat from time to time on the infrequent stances.
What height had we gained? Perhaps 800 feet—1,000
feet at the most! We were not far from the 20,000-foot
level, but we had still another 3,000 feet to go. If the

difficulties continued, how long was it going to take to get to the top?

I asked Robert, who was lying beside me, what he thought:

"In my opinion," he replied, "we've done the worst. We're in the séracs; tomorrow the Upper Glacier will take us very high, and after that there are only snow slopes, which will always 'go'. I think that by the afternoon of the day after tomorrow we shall be there."

Adrien and Lucien agreed, also Pierre, but with the reservation "if the séracs go all right". Edmond said he was ready for anything, if only somebody would give him some food!

Now that we were warm once more, we turned to thoughts of food and drink.

Robert filled the two cookers and melted snow. By the time we had consumed half a tinful of soup and a couple of pints of Ovomaltine it was past midnight. We had scarcely drunk the last mouthful before we dozed off into an uneasy slumber.

Chapter Four

VICTORY AT LAST

February 24th, 5 a.m.

BY a curious coincidence we all awoke at the same time, as though by a presentiment of evil. We were greeted by a wan light and a milky sky, and a huge pale-green cloud fringed with grey was passing slowly overhead. In spite of the wind blowing over the top of the South Summit, it appeared to be almost stationary, and rather like some evil spirit lying in wait for its victim. This monstrous bat-like apparition did not seem to be affected by air currents and we watched its progress with mixed feelings. The wind blowing from the direction of the Pacific coupled with the advent of this unprepossessing cloud were undoubtedly signs of bad weather to come. The wind was tearing away the snow from the South Summit in huge plumes and carrying it far into the upper atmosphere, where it spread like a transparent curtain over the heavens.

"Have you seen the sky?"

"Yes, it looks like a bad storm."

The silence which followed seemed all the more poignant, and everybody realised the seriousness of the situation. Our previous efforts, the fatigue to which we had been subjected and the risks we had run up to now, were they all in vain? We had to make a momentous choice. If we gave up, we would abandon all hope of victory, for we would never return to the Face; on the other hand if we went on it would mean total war.

This was a decision of great moment, for the choice before us today might no longer be possible tomorrow.

If the weather broke it would be too difficult and take too long to beat a retreat, and our only hope would be to reach the summit.

Quite apart from the 3,000 feet separating us from the top—3,000 feet of which we knew absolutely nothing—ought we to risk our lives on the somewhat chancy expectation of fine weather?

Silently we weighed up our chances and then somebody said:

"Well, what are we going to do?"

Pierre, always the cautious one, ventured: "There's no doubt that the weather outlook is bad; but often that doesn't mean a thing, and perhaps the next day . . ."

"That's quite true," said Adrien encouragingly. "I know that all these signs and portents, and especially the cirrus clouds, mean no good, but I have seen it just like this at Chamonix, and in spite of all it stayed fine for a fortnight. Guy, do you remember 1949 . . ."

"Yes, I remember. The wind was in the west with the foehn cap on Mont Blanc, but nevertheless we had a fortnight's fine weather."

"And what's more," added Edmond, "it would be most unprecedented for the weather to break up suddenly after such a long fine spell. I think it'll hold tomorrow and just give us time to get up."

"In other words," concluded Robert, "there's really no problem at all; everyone is agreed, so we go!"

"Pardon me," replied Lucien, "I haven't said anything yet. Everybody's agreed, O.K.! But not me!!"

He said this with such emphasis that for a moment we did not realise that he was joking.

"Kindly reserve your energy for melting snow, instead of for making bad jokes," said Robert caustically. "Come on, boys; we've got to get cracking and get the hell out of here!"

Once having made our decision, we began to get ready.

While Lucien and Robert boiled some water, we sorted out all unnecessary equipment. From now on we would make do with one cooker; in any case there was not enough fuel for both.

Our boots were frozen stiff, and it took some time to soften them by putting them in our sleeping-bags. Everyone drank a little warm water, to which a dose of coramine had been added. At eight o'clock we put on our crampons, roped up and started off to tackle the séracs.

I left first, with Lucien on my rope. No sooner had we passed the huge sérac at the foot of which we had spent the night than the ice slope steepened and became littered with enormous blocks fallen from the snout of the glacier above. We had to find a way through this ice labyrinth, criss-crossed by huge crevasses which forced us to make a number of détours. Now and again a thin tongue of ice formed a fragile bridge, which we crossed with the utmost care. The sun had chased away the morning mist, but the wind was still blowing hard on the glacier. The queer cloud seemed to keep pace with us, for it was still there, floating along over our heads.

The snout of the glacier rose above us, presenting a vertical wall about 150 feet high. It looked as though it had been cut with a knife. It was quite smooth and absolutely perpendicular, and defied all attempt to scale it. We made a diagonal traverse to the right on some fragile snow-ledges towards a gigantic fault which formed a sort of re-entrant in the ice. As we advanced into the angle we reached a ledge where the whole party assembled.

The snow of the Upper Glacier shone in the morning sun, but we were separated from it by a vertical wall of ice some 60 feet in height. Like animals caught in a trap, we made a careful survey of the surrounding walls. The fault terminated in a huge ice grotto leading deep into the heart of the glacier, from the roof of which hung fantastic stalactites. The left wall ended in a cornice several feet high, embellished with icicles, and behind us the edges of this enormous crevasse formed a large U, through which we had entered. We turned to the right wall, which was the only way left.

"That's all right," said Lucien simply; "all it needs is some ice pitons and étriers—I'm off!"

Bristling with steel and belayed on the doubled rope, he climbed up a few feet and inserted a piton. We waited in silence, which was broken only by the whirring of Adrien's ciné-camera.

More pitons and étriers, and he began to make slow progress. When about half-way up he turned, out of breath, and, hanging from a piton by one hand, said:

"I can't make it, chaps; it's ruddy awful. I've got cramp in the arms."

"Come on down," said Robert. "I'll take over."

We took in the rope as he descended very slowly. Robert started off.

"Be careful," warned Lucien, "the ice is not consolidated up above: it's rotten and the pitons won't hold."

The top layer was not pure ice, but a sort of uncompacted névé—not solid enough to take pitons. Robert got over this difficult portion by thrusting in three axes which he used as a kind of ladder. They wavered under his weight, but held just enough to allow him to get his arms over the top and pull himself up by crawling up the snow of the glacier. Adrien, who had never stopped filming, shouted to him to stand upright so that he should be silhouetted against the skyline. He did not reply, which was hardly surprising, as he was lying flat on the snow and his left arm, hanging free, was raised and lowered in a gesture of refusal and exhaustion.

He remained thus for several moments without moving, and then, supporting himself on his forearms, he raised his head. We could hear his stertorous breathing quite plainly. He turned towards us and a smile lit up his strained face:

ARTIFICIAL CLIMBING ON ICE AT 20,000′

"It's O.K.; we've done it!"

"No kidding, what can you see? What's it like?"

"Wait a tick: I'm out of breath. The glacier is quite flat, and I have the impression that it's not much farther, the summit is visible; it's terrific!"

We wanted to see as well, and after hauling up the sacks, rapidly climbed the pitch. As last on the rope, I pulled out the pitons (by hand!), and could not refrain from smiling to myself to think that my friends had entrusted their lives to these flimsy safety devices.

Once on top of the fault we took stock of the situation. The glacier ascended in a gentle slope to the foot of the final surge upwards of the Face, and for the first time it seemed as though the mountain had at last relented.

The contrast between the previous pitch and the snow slope ahead made us feel optimistic. We had so often said: "Once on the Upper Glacier and we've won!", that unconsciously our judgement had let us down and we had been tricked by the mountain. Carried away by our delight at having got so far, we failed to realise that there were still about 3,000 feet to be climbed, equivalent to one of the great Alpine faces, and that at a height of over 20,000 feet. Moreover, we had only just managed to escape from the very jaws of a trap.

The snow was exceedingly soft, and we sank in up to our waists, having to dig a trench through the floury substance. Lucien was leading and soon stopped and bent his head over his axe. When I got up to him he turned and said:

"It ruddy well would! It's the first time for more than a month that we've come across an easy slope, and it had to be new snow!"

Our pace was now desperately slow, for the snow would not bear. Every fifty feet or so I had to lean my head on my axe with my lungs on fire in order to snatch a few moments' rest. The nearer we got to the final wall, the better could we perceive its formidable defences. We had hoped to ascend a great snow couloir between the two summits, but it was a vain hope. The slope did not connect with the glacier, but was separated from it by a zone of smooth slabs, polished by ice avalanches. This section which was quite unclimbable completely cut across the Face for a distance of about 2,500 feet. There was only one possible solution, a very steep rock rib starting about 1,000 feet to the right of the fall-line of the North Summit and slanting obliquely to the North Arête. Once again we had no choice in the matter, and we directed our steps towards the foot of this rib.

We made frequent changes in the lead, and the hours slipped by all too quickly. We had left the séracs at 1 p.m., and had been forcing our laborious way through the deep snow for more than six hours. Edmond complained of the cold, and our feet, constricted by the crampon straps, had no feeling left in them. We reached the rib at 7.30 p.m., and as we were quite exhausted, we decided to bivouac in a large crevasse.

We all huddled together, while Robert tried to melt some snow. By comparison with the neighbouring peaks we estimated that our height was somewhere about 21,000 feet.

"We haven't made much height today," grumbled Pierre.

"Oh, I don't know," replied Adrien, "we've climbed 1,600 feet and passed through the séracs; surely that's something! That only leaves another 2,000 feet, and we'll do that tomorrow, even if we have to finish it by night."

"Yes, but that depends on the bergschrund just above," said Lucien.

"I agree with Adrien," said I; "the bergschrund will only take an hour at the most, and after that we'll make very rapid going up the ice slope. In any event, the North Arête is now quite close."

"Whatever happens, we've got to go all out," said

Robert; "it's taking a hell of a time—I suppose you know the fuel is running out very quickly."

I asked Edmond, who was already in his sleeping-bag: "What's your opinion?"

"Oh, you know I agree. At the moment I haven't got a very clear opinion about anything; I'm so beastly cold."

"Your feet?"

"Feet and hands."

"Now look, you've got to do something about that. Bang your feet together and rub your hands. Everybody pay attention, please. Look out for frostbite. As soon as the water is ready, I'm going to dish out some coramine to take with it; that'll leave one more dose for tomorrow morning."

Lucien hummed a samba in time with the tapping of our feet on the ice. At last we were able to take a few mouthfuls of tepid water, which tasted delicious, but was not nearly enough. We were so thirsty that even the cold took second place.

Night had fallen as we congregated round the tiny blue flame of the cooker. I made myself swallow two squares of nougat. The cooker had gone out as Robert passed round the tin of Ovomaltine—three mouthfuls each, not more! Our last signal flare had got broken in the sack and could not be used. We threw it away, and it rolled down the slope and disappeared from view.

I woke with a start at the feel of snow on my face. I had the impression that an icy hand was clutching my heart. Snow, bad weather, that was the end! I looked upwards, and could see the stars and a small crescent moon hanging over the North Arête. Never before had stars looked so beautiful. The moon was rather miserable, more like a painting done by a bad amateur; but it was there, spreading its friendly light over our world of ice and snow.

Moon and stars—then the weather hadn't broken? But where was the snow coming from which was whirling round in the tent and penetrating into my sleeping-bag? The night was alive with its rustling. What did it all mean? Half conscious, I must have spoken aloud, for Lucien answered me:

"It's the wind; don't you understand? It must be what they call the *viento blanco* [white wind]."

"Yes, that's it—the wind. I thought the weather had broken."

"But it isn't too good, anyhow. If it doesn't stop before dawn, we won't all get to the top, even supposing we all start!"

I buried my head in the hood of my sleeping-bag and looked at my watch. One o'clock; another five hours before dawn. Lucien was a pessimist. I refused to believe that the weather had gone back on us.

February 24th, 6 a.m.

The wind was blowing in gusts, raising clouds of snow on the Upper Glacier. We were buried beneath a deep layer of powder snow, but the sky was blue and flecked with clouds.

It was Adrien's turn at cooking, and this normal and rather humdrum occupation was today transformed into a really hard task.

At the prevailing low temperature the fuel resolutely refused to ignite, so Adrien was obliged to warm the container in his sleeping-bag for a long time before he was able to get the cooker going. Altogether it took him an hour and a half to melt a tinful of snow. When he had finished he looked rather like a husky, for his breath had condensed and deposited a coating of hoar frost on the hood of his anorak, giving him a halo of white "fur".

The tin was passed round, and as I was at the end of the queue, when it reached me the liquid was covered with a thin sheet of ice which I had to break before I could drink. During "breakfast" the snow bridge on which we were sitting suddenly cracked ominously:

"Ah," said Edmond quietly, "if it goes on like that we'll soon be in the basement! That really would be the limit; we've had enough of this blasted Face as it is!"

We made hurried preparations to start, without further comment. I got my boots out of my sack with the utmost caution—one false move might result in a boot shooting down the mountain never to be seen again, and that would be equivalent to a sentence of death! I hugged my precious footgear to myself inside my sleeping-bag in order to soften the leather. This turned out to be a waste of time, for no sooner had we put them down on the ice than the sudden change in temperature gave them a thick coating of frost on the inside. Before putting them on we had to scrape away what we could with a rock piton.

We finally left our crevasse at 8.15 a.m. I led up a very steep ice slope, and after two run-outs we got on to the lower lip of the schrund separating us from the ice couloir which we intended to climb in order to reach the crest of the rib. We crossed a zone of ice-blocks mixed with rock islands while the blizzard whipped against our nylon outer garments with a continuous crackling sound. After a good look at the upper lip about fifty feet above us, Lucien said:

"Well, it's no use messing about—I'm going. Belay me, please."

I dug my axe well into the snow.

"O.K., I'm ready. What are you going to do? Are you going straight up or over to the right between the rock and the snow?"

"I'm going to the right; it looks less steep."

He traversed a few yards, and then returned diagonally until he was directly above me, digging his crampons into the ice and using minute cracks in the rock as handholds. With extreme care he cut a few steps in a thin tongue of ice and reached the base of a small vertical rock wall.

"Guy, you've got to come and belay me, quick!"

"Right, take in the slack. I won't go your way—I'll come straight up."

Lucien leaned outwards and said:

"Just as you like. I think it'll 'go,' but watch your step—you're only belayed round a small rock-knob; it isn't much good and I can't knock in a piton."

Held on a tight rope, I managed to reach the tiny stance which he had cut in the ice. We were now in the shadow of the rib, and the rock froze our hands through our gloves. The others were waiting impatiently thirty feet below, hopping from one foot to another to keep warm. For a few moments a more than usually violent gust flattened us against the rock; our friends had disappeared, enveloped in blinding clouds of driving snow. Taking advantage of a sudden calm spell, Lucien attacked the wall. He managed to struggle up a few yards and then stopped and, turning his head, said:

"I'm coming down—my hands are too cold. And for God's sake watch out: I've just about had it, I may come off."

If he did come off, I could not possibly hold him—the belay was too small. He would pull me off my holds, and we would both fall down to the edge of the crevasse thirty feet below.

It was a curious thing, but I was able to contemplate this possibility quite serenely and without any fear at all. I watched Lucien's every move, but with a sort of complete detachment. It wouldn't have taken much for me to have said, "Come on, Lulu; you're not in form today; pull yourself together—you can climb it."

He rejoined me on the ice, quite out of breath. With an almost supernatural calm, I said to him:

"Have a breather, while I take a crack at it."

I looked at the holds, took off my gloves and pulled myself up to the point reached by Lucien. Three or four yards higher up the sun was shining on the ice-slope, but

I just couldn't make it. My fingers refused to grip the rocks, do what I would: it was as if somebody had hit me hard on the wrists. All my late confidence evaporated in a flash, and I had to come down.

Gasping for air, I said to Lucien:

"It just won't 'go' with crampons."

"How right you are. Help me to take them off."

It took us ten minutes to unstrap his crampons. He thrust his hands in his pockets to warm them, took a deep breath, raised his head, and said:

"Right!"

We looked at one another for a minute:

"Lulu, you've got to do it."

"Don't worry, I'll get up."

Now that he was no longer wearing crampons I was able to help him by giving him a shoulder. He stood upright on my shoulders, blew on his fingers and said shortly:

"Are you ready? I'm going."

With outstretched arms I held his feet to give him a start. His right foot left my hand and then his left. I could do nothing more for him except wish him the best of luck. Two pull-ups in succession, and he planted his axe in the snow with a shout of triumph. I fastened his crampons on to the rope and sent them up to him. After putting them on he climbed up a few feet, dug his axe in firmly and shouted "That's it; I can hold you now. Bring up the others."

I turned and asked the others to be patient for a few more minutes until I had warmed my hands. When I took off my gloves, my heart sank into my boots: my hands were completely white, the fingers looking like birds' claws and quite useless. In a panic I remembered those awful photographs of Maurice Herzog's hands. (*Translator's Note:* In the course of the successful ascent of Annapurna, Herzog lost all his fingers and toes and Lachenal all his toes.) Then I got busy. I stuck my gloves under my armpits beneath my down coat and hit the rock with my hands with all my strength for several minutes, after which I put them in my pockets and waited. At the end of five minutes, excruciating pain told me that the circulation was beginning to return. Before putting on my gloves again I tested my restored fingers by nibbling at them. All was well; but only just in time!

Thanks to Lucien's help we all climbed the pitch, but when we were finally all assembled on the slope above we found that we had taken five hours to do sixty feet!

The North Arête was now very close, but we knew that we should not reach it that evening. Slowly, step by step, we ascended the steep couloir. Fortunately the wind had dropped and we were in the sun, but we were tortured by intense thirst. At the end of each run-out we melted a little snow in our mouths with a mint tablet. This was only a stopgap, and the burning thirst returned worse than ever. At six o'clock we had reached the start of the rib. The slope ended abruptly with a short corniced ridge. We hastily cut a small shelf on which to put down the sacks. A few yards higher up a narrow chimney marked the start of the rock rib. Lucien made an appreciation of the pitch and then said:

"It doesn't look too bad, but I think it would be better to fix a rope; it'll save time in the morning. We can spend the night here provided we can find a good spot in the rocks."

Robert, who had just arrived, agreed with him.

"Are you both going? Meanwhile I'll start the platform with the others."

"Good!" said Lucien. "We'll leave the sacks here and Guy and I will go on. But before I start I'd like to have a look at my left hand; that cut on my finger's hurting." He took off his glove. "My God, look at my hand!"

His fingers were twice the usual size, violet in colour

168

and covered with huge blisters. Only the thumb was normal. He stared at his hand with a look of horror.

"My hand's done for; it's just like Maurice Herzog's."

I reassured him while I pulled off the bandage.

"Nonsense! If you remember, Maurice's fingers had burst. All you've got is a severe local frostbite, quite superficial."

"Maybe you're right; that would explain the blisters." He shrugged his shoulders, "Anyhow, it's done, and that's that."

He put on his glove and said:

"Well, let's go; we'll take an extra 'two hundred' feet [200-foot rope] with us."

"Would you like me to lead?"

"No; now that the bandage is off, I'll be all right."

At the end of an hour and a half we had fixed two ropes on the ridge. The rocks were steep and icy and difficult throughout—the mountain was not giving anything away! We slid down the ropes and joined the others on the unfinished platform. Adrien, who was stamping down the snow, was surprised to see us.

"What! You're back already? Couldn't you find anywhere to sleep up there?"

"Not a hope," replied Lucien; "it's very steep and not a sign of a platform of any sort."

"Yes, but one can always find somewhere or other in rocks," retorted Adrien, "you just didn't look properly."

"Look here," said Lucien aggressively. "If you think we're clots, why not say so! I tell you there was absolutely nothing. Is that quite clear?"

"What's biting you? There isn't room for six here—at the most only for two or three. I'm browned off with the snow, and I'm going to have a look for myself. Are you coming with me, Pierre?"

Pierre allowed himself to be persuaded, and they both put on their sacks and began to climb up the ropes. Lucien looked at me and shrugged his shoulders:

"Let them go, if it amuses them!"

Trembling with cold, we set to work on the snow cornice. Fortunately the snow was fairly easy to shift and we scooped out a sort of dug-out about three feet deep—just enough to shelter our heads and shoulders. We also made a narrow ledge in the ice of the slope, in the course of which we broke an ice-axe haft. When it was large enough for the four of us we slid into our bivouac tent and tried to get warm again. Falling stones and fragments of conversation announced the return of Pierre and Adrien. Obviously they had found nowhere to spend the night in the rocks.

"So you've already settled down," said Adrien in a dead voice. "What about Pierre and I?"

"You'll have to look out for yourselves; there's hardly room for four here."

In a dull sort of way I realised that we were behaving rather like animals fighting for their lives—everyone for himself. It was a bad sign. Anyhow, why did they bother about their beastly rocks in the first place?

We heard scraps of conversation followed by sounds of ice being cut with the axe and the clear, vibrant noise of an ice piton going in. Time passed and warmth returned to us, so that we could once more speak and act. Robert set up the cooker, placing the burner in a tin to reduce the loss of heat. I looked out and could see that Pierre and Adrien had cut out a seat for the two of them a few feet away from us. They were sitting with their backs to the cornice and their legs hanging down the slope. Night was coming on, and the first stars began to make their appearance, while a small crescent moon could be seen just above the North Arête. The cooker went out, and Robert lifted the top:

"Just about a third of a tinful. What shall we do—carry on or leave a little for a drink tomorrow morning?"

We decided to keep back a little fuel for breakfast. Robert diluted the water with a little snow powder and a pinch of tea dust; I kept my sip of liquid in my mouth for a long time before swallowing it.

Every time anyone moved, the tent tightened up like a net and pulled me up against Edmond. We tried to find more comfortable positions, but the slightest movement called forth a storm of protests. Eventually I tore a hole in the tent so as to get a little air.

In order to assuage our terrible thirst we had put a spoon in the snow above our heads, and in turn we scraped a spoonful of snow which we sprinkled with tea-dust before swallowing it.

I dozed off and dreamed that I was engaged in under-water fishing. I was chasing an enormous fish when my breath failed and I had to fight my way to the surface. I thrashed the water in desperation and awoke to hear Edmond telling me not to be so restless, as I was keeping him awake!

"I'm sorry, I was dreaming."

"Of what?"

"Oh, holidays, Corsica, the yellow sand burning in the sun, the blue glittering sea, the lovely Mediterranean lighting . . . and here we are in the ice at 22,000 feet!"

"Oh yes. Do you remember Rio? That was a nice spot too."

I lingered over the memories of the hot days of the voyage when suddenly a thought struck me:

"Edmond, do you remember the night we left Rio and I wanted to show you the Southern Cross through the port-hole? You couldn't be bothered to get out of your bunk. Well, you can see it now without any trouble at all, it's just over there, and there's no port-hole in the way!"

He laughed.

"I remember it very well. I was sweltering in my bunk in spite of the fans. . . . What a ruddy life!"

We sipped a spoonful of snow and tea, which for a moment soothed our cracked lips.

Outside Pierre and Adrien, wrapped in their grey bivouac clothing, looked like a couple of mediæval gargoyles.

"How's it going, Didi?"

One of the shapes moved slightly and a hooded head turned towards me:

"Oh, all right; but don't move about too much in that tent, or you'll have us all down the slope. You might at least have tied yourselves on!"

This was only too true: our legs were hanging down and we were liable to slip at any moment. On the other hand, the heat of our bodies had frozen the canvas on to the ice. I calculated that this regelation was sufficient to hold us in position so I replied airily: "Don't worry, we shan't slide off; we're frozen in!"

In vain I tried to sleep. Hardly had I dozed off before I awoke with a feeling of suffocation. Edmond was groaning softly; he shuddered and looked at me with astonishment.

I said to him quietly, "Pity to wake up."

He nodded and sighed: "Oh Lord, I'm thirsty."

I stretched out my arm and scratched the snow; as we had now got down to the ice, the spoon broke off short. We all had to turn over so that I could search in my pocket for another. The spoon passed from mouth to mouth.

"It doesn't come up to half a bitter!" remarked Robert. This sentence fell like a cube of ice into a dry martini!

Beer . . . the thick brown beer which one gets in the estaminets of Alsace in small stone mugs wet with dew. . . . To have a large pint tankard in the hand full to the brim with the amber liquid and topped with effervescing froth, running over down the side!

"When one thinks of all the possible drinks!" said Lucien reminiscently. "When we get down we'll drink the lot—beer, wine, whisky, fruit juice—until we bust!"

"As for me," said Robert, "I'm a beer-drinker; there's nothing like beer when you're really thirsty."

With closed eyes each of us dreamed of his own particular drink and strove to remain oblivious of the thirst and cold. Time seemed suspended and I tried not to look at my watch in order to keep up the illusion.

Edmond murmured in a low voice:

"I'm thinking of a room in the country with a huge log fire, you know those logs which collapse with a shower of sparks . . . and a girl sitting in front of the fire and me lying on the ground with my head on her knee. . . ."

These words conjured up a lovely vision. I could see the dancing flames, the graceful silhouette, her long hair reflecting the light. I couldn't see her face, but I knew that she was smiling at me. I could feel the warmth of her body when she put her head on my shoulder and snuggled up close to me. . . .

And here we were, alone in this world of ice and rock, sitting on the ice at nearly 23,000 feet of our own free will, when there were so many soft warm nights all over the world!

Why were we here in this trap which we had prepared for ourselves day by day? Why did we always fight against the world, instead of taking advantage of the peace it offered? If we were here it was not because we were strong; on the contrary, it was because we were not sure what we wanted, unless it was simply submission to some unknown law.

The sky lightened slowly, dawn gradually extinguished the stars and the frost penetrated like a knife. We filled the burner for the last time and managed to boil about an inch of water in the bottom of the tin, to which we periodically added spoonfuls of snow. This worked quite well, for by the time the cooker had gone out the tin was about half full.

173

Adrien and Pierre, who were starting first, got ready slowly. Suddenly Robert turned round and was violently sick.

"Robert, old chap," I said anxiously, "what's the matter? Are you ill?"

He shook his head. "No, it's nothing; it'll pass. It's just a nervous reaction; it's happened to me before in the Alps."

"What a wicked waste of tea!" said Lucien with mock dejection.

Robert's colour began to come back gradually.

"I think I should like you to give me some coramine."

"There's no more to drink; I can only give you an injection."

"All right, let's have a stab; only don't butcher me."

In spite of our awkward position (we were still in bed and he had to stretch his arm out over Edmond), the operation was successful. The sun was slowly coming down the rib; it was already eight o'clock, and high time to start.

As soon as we had got our boots on we made a rigid check of our remaining equipment, and retained only our down jackets and bivouac clothing. Robert spread out the double roof of the tent on the ice, hoping that its yellow colour could be seen from Base Camp. A kick sent the cooker bouncing down the slope, followed by the fuel container and the broken axe. We took pitons, étriers and spare rope rings out of our sacks, which, together with an electric lamp, and empty tins of Ovo-maltine, made a fine pile of bric-à-brac. After a moment's hesitation, Pierre and I added our snow-gaiters to this collection. That was the lot. The lighter we were the sooner we would get there.

Pierre and Adrien started up the ropes fixed last night, followed by Robert and Edmond. Lucien and I came last.

"Will your hand be all right, Lulu?"

"It'll have to be. Don't worry, it's only my fore-finger, and I can still use it."

One by one we clambered up the two chimneys equipped with ropes the night before. Higher up the rib rose in a series of steep steps for several run-outs; then it widened and disappeared in a face of very steep broken rock covered with ice and snow. The rib did not join the arête! Like a hunted animal, I eagerly sought for a way out.

It was impossible to climb the face direct: we could not do it in our present state of fatigue. To the left the wall of séracs was completely overhanging: there was no exit that way. All that was left was a series of snow-ledges on the right; they looked extremely formidable, but they would have to do. When Lucien came up to me, I vented my wrath on this blasted Face which refused to let up and defended itself to the very last.

"Just look at it: hard going right to the very end! It's a real basket!"

Lucien slowly surveyed the pitch and then said:

"Never mind; we'll climb up to the right, up the snow."

We went on. Run-out monotonously followed run-out in very difficult ground. The cracks and crannies in the rocks were all blocked with snow and ice. Lucien and I caught up Robert and Edmond and overtook them. It was already past midday. Adrien had been leading since we started this morning—it was time we relieved him. I got level with Pierre:

"How's it going, Pierrot?"

"I'm a bit tired; otherwise O.K."

"Let me go on; I'll take over from Didi."

"Righto. I say, Guy, can you give me a stab of coramine? It seems to have done Robert a spot of good."

We reached a small stance a few feet higher, where there was room for two. While Pierre belayed Adrien, who was coping with the next step in the ridge, I prepared the syringe.

I got out the glass capsule and broke off the end. The liquid was frozen, but I got over this by putting the capsule in my mouth to warm it. I filled the syringe, breathed on the needle and quickly pricked Pierre in the forearm.

Adrien, who was about fifty feet above us, turned round and said briskly: "Come on; only another run-out and we're on the snow."

I climbed the pitch. It ended in a deep fissure like those one finds in the Chamonix Aiguilles—a tough climb involving lay-backs and much wriggling. At this height too—we seemed to be spared nothing!

I asked Adrien if I should take over the lead. He replied, smiling:

"I'll just do another run-out; after that, if you want to tackle the snow slope, you can have it."

"That suit's me. You've often told me that I'm the ice expert. . . . I'll deal with the slopes."

The rib thinned out and finally disappeared and we had to traverse 150 feet of ice-glazed rock to the right before we got to the snow. Now came the slopes—undoubtedly steep; but, after all, still slopes which would "go". Three hundred feet above was the arête, it was the last lap.

Three o'clock. I became impatient and could wait no longer.

"Didi, I'm starting the traverse. Do you realise it's three o'clock?"

He shrugged his shoulders. "Keep calm; we must wait for them."

Lucien reached the lower stance, and Robert and Pierre were moving together below him, Edmond bringing up the rear.

I didn't wait any longer; and, unroped, I started the traverse and reached the first slope, where I cut a little platform and put on my crampons. Sitting back on my sack I lit a cigarette and waited for my friends. I was in the sun, and the precipitous slope shot down below my feet. For the first time during the ascent of the Face I experienced that feeling of calm and relaxation which invariably precedes the "exit" from a great face when one is sure of victory. My feet were very cold—the same old story, one can never put on crampons without getting one's feet half frozen.

Five o'clock. I kicked my toes into the hard snow. The slope was so steep that I had a job to keep my balance when pulling out my axe in order to put it in higher up. I had never climbed anything as steep as this —the angle must have been about 70°—but fortunately the hard snow was just right for crampon work.

We were now in the shade of a rock buttress, and the cold was so intense that it tightened the skin at the corners of my mouth, and my hands were quite numb. But nothing mattered now. I could see the sun shining on a small rock island sixty feet above, and this island was standing out against the skyline. I suddenly realised what that signified: it meant that that rock was on the arête, the culminating point of the South Face.

Step by step I crept slowly upwards. At last I was able to put my hands on the rock and hoist myself up. The sun shone on me from my waist up. I HAD REACHED THE ARÊTE.

I was suddenly assailed by a depressing thought, for I couldn't believe that the mountain had really capitulated. Perhaps there still remained an insurmountable obstacle—another rock face? I carefully examined the arête. It stretched away in front of me sloping gently upwards in the sunshine. There was no further impediment.

I turned towards my companions, who were visible as bright spots of colour against the enamel blue of the slope.

"It's all over. We've won!"

The uttering of these few words made something break inside me, and I couldn't help crying impotently. I had cold hands, I was fed up and wished that it really was all over.

I took in Lucien's rope, and this simple action had a calming effect on me. When he joined me on the ridge, he too burst into tears.

"Oh, Guy, forgive me. It's damn silly, but I'm crying like a kid!"

"That's all right. I did the same five minutes ago; it's just nervous reaction. Come on; bring up Adrien, while I just go on to the saddle above."

From the crest of the arête we could see the Pacific slope of Aconcagua. This was a good description of the North side of the mountain, which descends in a series of well-graded steps and plateaux. There was virtually no snow at all, and it was difficult to believe that we were at a height of over 20,000 feet.

While the second rope (Robert, Pierre and Edmond) was climbing up to the arête, Lucien, Adrien and I started off along the ridge. We mounted the first ice hump, but were going too fast for Adrien, who had to stop for breath. The tightened rope pulled Lucien up short, and he in turn pulled on the rope between us. At the third enforced halt, Lucien let fly at Adrien:

"Don't keep stopping, Didi; it's a little wearing just at the end!"

Adrien replied:

"Good Lord! It's all over and I want to go along at my own pace and what's more I don't see why I should stay roped at all. If you want to gallop, I won't stop you!"

He unroped, fuming. Leaning on my axe, I watched the little scene in silence. There was no longer any risk and basically he was quite right to take off the rope.

We went on our way. After the ice hump came an

expanse of snow-covered scree, followed by a second hump. I assumed that this must be the last rise before the actual summit. I waited a moment for Lucien.

"You see that dark line over there. That must be the Pacific," he said.

"Yes, I think you're right. It must lie over there somewhere. Come on: it's half-past seven. We haven't too much time."

Step by step we tramped over the wind-driven surface of the ice, and then quite suddenly there was no more snow. The arête broadened and became a stony plateau, on which we walked with difficulty owing to our crampons.

We must be at the top, somewhere there was a cairn; it was not visible but Réné had told me there was one.

A few more feet and there, just round a rise, was a cross and an aluminium table about three feet high. A little in front, and below the table, were two dark figures.

As we drew nearer we recognised the busts of President and Eva Peron. She was on his left, and both faced the South Face, with their backs to the Pacific.

Intrigued, we approached the table, but before reaching it I stumbled over a supporting wire. The thought of falling over a guy-rope at 23,000 feet on the summit of the two Americas amused me childishly. We unroped and took off our crampons. We were able to move about with greater ease now that we were free of the rope.

There was a drawer in the table, but it was padlocked. I was just about to force it with my axe when I saw through a little window let into the top of the table that it was empty. Lucien called me over:

"Guy, I've discovered a book. Fancy that! What organisation!" We turned over the pages.

"I can't understand a word," said he—"it's all in Spanish. What shall we do? Shall we add something?"

"Oh, what's the good? Anyhow, have you got a pencil?"

"No."

"Neither have I. That settles it."

We replaced the book in its iron box and put a stone on the cover.

Our eyes strayed down the precipices of the South Face. It was a funny thing, but we were not happy. The victory which we had just pulled off did not awake any echo in our hearts.

I was suddenly overcome with fatigue, we had been waiting so eagerly for this moment of success for which we had fought day and night for so long, that its achievement was a sort of anti-climax. Lucien said quietly:

"Well, we've done it, we've made the first ascent of the South Face of Aconcagua."

"Yes, after all, that's what we came here for!"

Chapter Five

THE DESCENT

Lucien was leaning against the aluminium table, coiling up the rope. As I watched him I suddenly became aware of the strong wind and intense cold. Shivering, I said to him:

"It's eight o'clock and it's ruddy cold; there's nothing more to do up here; let's get on out of it."

"I quite agree, but what about the others?"

We took a few steps along the summit platform and looked down the North Arête. About 500 feet away, Adrien was coming along slowly bending over his axe. A little lower down we could see the other three silhouetted against the sky.

"There you are," said Lucien; "they're coming; they'll be here in a quarter of an hour."

"All right, but we won't stop on the summit, we'll get down a bit into the 'canaleta', at least we'll be out of the wind there."

We picked up our sacks and started off down the north side. The "canaleta" was a sort of scree couloir, quite easy, starting down from the ridge uniting the North and South summits of the mountain. 150 feet lower down we stopped and lit a cigarette in the shelter of a large rock. A few moments later, Adrien appeared on the summit. We hailed him:

"Here we are, Didi; are you coming down?"

"Not yet, I'm going to wait for the others and film their arrival on the summit."

"Will you be long?"

"No, about five minutes; they're just coming."

"Righto, we'll go on ahead and look for the hut."

"O.K., so long."

We continued the descent, trying to keep to the track of the normal route. We quickly lost height, and soon we saw a mule-track zig-zagging in front of us.

"It's just like the Plan des Aiguilles at Chamonix," said Lucien; "you'd never think we were 20,000 feet up."

It was quite true: compared to the incredibly steep

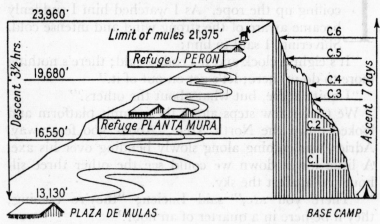

SKETCH MAP SHOWING BOTH SIDES OF ACONCAGUA
The six camps are marked on the South Face

face which we had just climbed, the gentle slopes of this side of the mountain reminded us forcibly of the alpine pastures of our own mountains. We had had so much to contend with in the course of the last few days that this descent seemed almost too easy. Full of suspicion, we recalled what Réné had said as he was describing the way down: "Don't go too low and don't get taken in by the easiness. Above all be sure not to miss the hut and don't get lost in the 'Relincho' for it's twenty-five miles to Inca."

Instead of following the tempting path, we traversed the moraine to the right. The evening was rapidly drawing on, and we scrutinised every rock with care so as to be sure of not missing the refuge. I tried to recollect the photos which Strouvé, the cinematographer of the Fitz-Roy expedition, had brought back showing the ordinary route up Aconcagua.

We contoured the base of the summit rocks, and every moment we thought we could see the hut. The wind had increased in violence, and I was obliged to shout at the top of my voice, although Lucien was only about fifty feet away.

In despair I caught up with him and said:

"In half an hour it'll be quite dark. It's just a waste of time looking for this blasted hut, let's find the path and get down as quickly as possible."

We glissaded down a snow slope to join the path. When we turned round we could just see the coloured anoraks of our friends through the gathering gloom. We now made rapid progress in spite of a strange sensation of stiffness in our legs, which we attributed to fatigue. The track mounted a rounded shoulder and Lucien, who was a few feet ahead of me, suddenly called out:

"There it is—really this time. I can see it, immediately below."

About 300 feet distant I could just make out a triangular shape on which were painted the blue-and-white colours of Argentina. Before descending the scree slope which separated us from the "Juan Peron" hut, we went back a little to shout the news to our friends.

The refuge was a sort of wooden "tent", about six feet square and five feet high. In his haste to open the door, Lucien nearly pulled it off its hinges. We crawled into the hut on all fours and I struck a match. The feeble light showed up the emptiness of the room. There was absolutely nothing there—no cooker, no fuel and no provisions.

We heard footsteps outside and Edmond and Pierre arrived.

"So this is the hut we've heard so much about," said Edmond; "at last we'll get something to drink."

"You've got another think coming," replied Lucien, "there's nothing here at all."

"What," said Robert, "surely the soldiers have been here."

"Come inside and look for yourself."

"We'd love to, if only Guy would get out of the way!"

I stepped to one side and Edmond entered carrying a tin of Ovomaltine.

"What are you doing with that?"

"It's the other half of the tin from this morning. I kept it because I thought I might find a stream in the 'canaleta'. When I found none, I added some snow; it's not a bad mixture. Will you try some?"

I shook my head. The thought of this glutinous paste in my dried-up throat was not to be endured.

We made a careful inventory of the hut. There was precious little to be found: a tin of condensed milk, a pint of fuel, and two or three empty meat tins. We managed to make a sort of cooker out of one of these tins, a few blows with an axe made holes for ventilation, a little fuel in the bottom and there it was! This contraption gave out very little heat and pungent fumes, but the snow with which we had filled another tin produced some brackish water which we drank with relish. We suddenly realised that there were only four of us. Where were Pierre and Adrien?

I asked Robert and Edmond:

"How is it that they're not here, for we saw Adrien before we left the summit?"

"I don't know," said Robert. "We all left the top together."

"Yes, it's funny," said Lucien; "we must do something about it."

Robert went in search of more snow and called loudly

for some time. He came in soon afterwards carrying a large block of ice.

"I yelled until I was blue in the face, but I don't think it carried far against the wind. I couldn't see them."

"But how did you get separated? What did you do on the summit?"

Robert replied:

"Nothing much. By the time we got to the ridge, you were about 500 feet in front of us. When we got to the summit, Adrien filmed us. I searched under the table and found the book under the stone."

Lucien interrupted him:

"So did we."

Robert went on in a superior tone:

"Ah, but you put nothing in it. I, on the other hand, wrote all our names, the date and the time with the caption, 'First ascent of the South Face'. Hats off, gentlemen!"

"Just because you've now learned to write," scoffed Edmond, "I thought you always signed your name with a cross!"

"Oh, you can laugh if you like, but I never thought it was so difficult to sharpen a pencil!"

We congratulated him on his presence of mind. He went on: "Well, I replaced the book while Pierre was coiling up the rope and we all came down together. We could see you two quite well in front, and, as you know, we got here just after you did. Frankly, I don't understand it."

While Lucien was looking after the cooker and melting the snow, Robert and I were busy with Edmond, who was complaining of his hands and feet. He took off his gloves: his fingers were swollen and blue.

"Do they hurt?" asked Robert.

"So so; it's the wool which irritates them."

I got out my red silk gloves which I had not used and helped him to put them on.

185

"I'm not worried about my hands; it's my feet, I can't feel them at all."

"Well, take your boots off, instead of talking about it," said Robert, "and let's have a look at your feet."

"I'd like to, but my hands hurt, so if it's not asking you too much, I'd be glad if you'd take them off for me," said Edmond with a smile.

We took off his boots and socks. Robert and I gazed at one another in silence. His feet were completely white as far as the ankles and streaked with blue.

He looked up, "Just what I thought—it's not so good."

In spite of the shock I got on seeing his feet, I felt it incumbent on me to say something:

"Don't worry, they only need rubbing and the circulation will come back."

Robert and I each took a foot and rubbed it vigorously. My hands were slightly frost-bitten, and the contact with his cold flesh was unbearable, I had to put on my woollen gloves before I could continue with the massage. The circulation of his toes was completely obstructed; the lower part of the foot was like a block of ice. We carried on with the massage for an hour without stopping. In the meantime, Lucien had contrived to melt half a tinful of warm water, which we shared among us. Then Robert said:

"We don't seem to be making much progress. Do you think it would be a good idea to beat them with a rope's end?"

In view of the state of his feet, we had nothing to lose in trying this, so we hit his feet very hard with rope loops in an attempt to restore circulation. By midnight our efforts were crowned with a certain amount of success, as he could now move his toes, which two hours before had seemed as hard and brittle as glass. We gave him a pair of dry socks and settled him down for the night.

We had by now abandoned any hope of seeing Pierre

and Adrien. While we were getting into our sleeping-bags, Lucien asked me:

"What do you think's happened to them?"

"Oh, there are two possibilities: either they've gone straight down to Plaza de Mulas or they're bivouacing. In any case, they've got all they want with them, so it's not serious."

"And what about Edmond's feet?"

"I don't like the look of them. Frankly, I've never seen anything like it. I'm afraid he'll lose them. What about your hand?"

"It's all right. A bit painful, perhaps. And you?"

"I think I've got a touch of frost in my feet. I'll have to watch out. They've burst; and we can't go to sleep until we've tried to get them back to something like normal."

"Apart from my left hand, I'm not worrying at all. I just feel a bit languid as one does sometimes when ski-ing."

"Well, take care, we're still at 21,300 feet, and it would be just plain stupid to get caught here now that it's all over."

Together we beat our feet in time against the sloping roof; fighting desperately against an irresistible desire to sleep. I said to Edmond:

"Try to move your toes all you can and above all don't go to sleep."

I had no feeling in my feet and I kept on beating them against the hut. Lucien dozed off with his head on my shoulder. I shook him awake.

"Remember your feet; don't go to sleep!"

"Blast my feet! they're all right. I'm too sleepy; let me be."

I went on mechanically banging my feet against the hut. I mustn't go to sleep—at least not yet, until my feet are right; it's too important. At half past one in the morning I finally gave up and went to sleep. We were in the hut, we had won and it was all over; and—ironically enough—for the first time I felt cold!

We were awakened by a ray of sunlight at 7.30 a.m. During the night the refuge had been transformed as if by magic. The condensation from our breath had covered the interior with a thick coat of frost, and we felt as though we were in a refrigerator. Lucien pushed open the door and the red sunlit rocks outside gave an impression of warmth. The sky was blue. We could not wait any longer—nobody would be coming up to look for us; it was time we got moving.

Robert went out in his socks and put all our boots in the sun to soften them up. At the end of a quarter of an hour we realised that in spite of the sunshine they would not thaw out in the prevailing low temperature.

"Nothing, doing. We'll have to put them on as they are. What do you think, Edmond, can you put yours on?"

"I'll damn well have to. I'm not going down in my socks."

I asked him: "How are your feet now?"

"Not so good. During the night my toes went solid again, but I can carry on, they don't hurt, I can't feel anything."

"You needn't worry if you can't get them on," said Lucien; "we can cut them open with a knife if necessary."

Robert went out and came back with the boots.

"Look," he said, "I've made a discovery."

He opened his hand and disclosed some peculiar-looking objects looking like bakelite.

"What on earth are those?" asked Lucien.

"Tinned apricots. Apparently there are people who have too much to eat; they must have thrown these away, for I found them scattered about among the rocks. They're completely frozen and as hard as wood."

We each took one and put them in our pockets to thaw them out for future use.

We got ready for the descent. I remembered that I had a spare pair of socks at the bottom of my sack, and put them under my shirt for a few minutes to warm them. My feet had no feeling and were quite white, but at least I could move all my toes. I was very sorry for Edmond and Lucien, for it was really all over now, and there was not much wrong with me. It was true I couldn't feel anything, but that had often happened to me before when ski-ing. I would soon get my circulation back on the way down. We packed up, cleaned up the hut and carefully closed the door.

The path wound down the mountain side at a comfortable angle, and in spite of our stiffened feet we made rapid progress.

For more than an hour we followed the windings of the path indicated by yellow marks, and soon perceived the two huts of Plantamura round a rock-spur. We were overjoyed to see tethered mules and people—in fact we could hardly believe our eyes. We started to run, taking short cuts down the scree and yelling at the top of our voices to signal our arrival.

When we got to the huts we were a little taken aback at seeing strangers, for we had expected to meet Sergeant Darvich and soldiers from the camp, but our welcome was none the less cordial.

The party consisted of two Chileans accompanied by an army sergeant an *arrierio** and a guide. The guide's name was Cassis. He was of Italian origin, and we were able to make ourselves understood in a mixture of that language and French.

We expressed astonishment at finding them there, and they explained that they belonged to the Argentine expedition "Feria de America" with Base Camp at Plaza

* An *arriero* is a horseman frequenting the Andes, part guide and part drover.

de Mulas, and that "Dallori and Lesour" (Adrien Dagory and Pierre Lesueur) had arrived there at half-past one in the morning. They had come to look for us and help us to descend. We thanked them, and asked them if by chance they had anything for us to drink. In a trice two thermos of hot coffee were produced and almost immediately emptied. We wished to go on down, and asked Cassis if they could take our sacks on their mules down to their camp. He replied with a smile that they could take us down as well—they had thought of everything!

"Is there anything to drink at Plaza de Mulas?"

"Anything you want."

"Then what are we waiting for? Let's go down at once!"

We got on our mules and commenced the descent. I have never professed to have much sympathy for these simple animals, but I must admit that it was very agreeable to be carried gently down the slope, comfortably seated on a sheepskin saddle and allowing the mule to find its own way, without having to think at all.

The *arriero* led the caravan. He was very curiously garbed: black trousers with grey stripes and a navy blue coat. Short boots and a cap with ear-pieces completed his equipment. When we came to a difficult section of the path he waited until my mule had got over it, encouraging it with curious clickings of the tongue and then turning to me with a warm smile.

I smiled back at him; it was good to feel isolated no longer and to be among human beings once more.

We now crossed an immense scree slope; in front of us the fine summit of Cuerno reared its snowy dome. The foot of the mountain was covered with huge penitentes, sparkling in the sunlight. Cassis had now ridden up, and he explained that the glacier ahead of us was the Upper Horcones Glacier, and that the large valley to the left was the Upper Horcones Valley. "Plaza de Mulas is over there," he said—"just by two little glacier lakes at the end of the glacier. We shall be there in an hour."

The scree slope eased off, and we were able to trot occasionally. We rounded a rocky rib and then saw the "tent village" of Plaza de Mulas a short distance away. As we were descending the last steep zig-zags, the sergeant went on ahead and shouted repeatedly: "Los Franceses—Congelados—Agua Caliente." (The Frenchmen—frostbite—hot water.)

At last we reached the camp. Everybody left their tents and crowded around us and willing arms stretched forward. I had considerable difficulty in getting them to let me get off my mule by myself. No sooner had my feet touched the ground than I was seized and borne aloft. What was the matter with them? Good Lord, I can stand up by myself!

After a few moments they all calmed down and, calling up all my limited knowledge of Spanish—chiefly consisting of *"Bueno"* and *"Muy bien"*—I managed to intimate that we were parched with thirst. Immediately various drinks were produced, such as fruit juice, soup, mineral water and tea, etc. Darvich and Raskin, whom we knew, fought their way through the crowd and embraced us. One of the two Chileans who had come to meet us spoke French and acted as our interpreter. We asked for news of Pierre and Adrien, and learned that they, too, were suffering from frostbite and had gone down to Inca this morning. Now that order had been restored I asked if somebody would look after Edmond and Lucien. Their boots were taken off and we saw that Edmond's feet were blue and that Lucien's toes were violet coloured.

They wanted to take off our boots as well, but at first we would not agree, as we were sure that we were all right. However, we gave way in the end, and Robert's feet turned out to be perfectly normal. I removed my first boot and had a great shock, the toes were all swollen and dark violet and the skin was shiny and velvety like a peach. I hastily took off the other boot, and found that the other foot was in the same condition.

I was shattered by this sight, but on second thoughts realised that all was not lost, and that perhaps we would come out of it better than we expected. I allowed two kindly attendants to massage my feet and turned to thoughts of food and drink.

Cassis asked me if we would like some wine! "What a question; of course we would. Bring it in!"

When they brought it we found that they had added hot water! The revolting mixture was quite undrinkable. Since our arrival everything they had given us to drink had been hot, which was quite all right in the case of fruit-juice. But wine, no! I endeavoured to explain to our friends that we wanted cold drinks more than anything, but they insisted that in our present condition we must have hot drinks. In the end somebody happened to say that the wine was tinned, so I resorted to cunning and asked to see a tin as a curiosity. As soon as one had been brought we seized it and drank its contents there and then, before they had a chance to heat it.

Everybody came to have a look at our feet and tried to tell us that it wasn't so serious after all. One of our Chilean friends said that frostbite was quite common on Aconcagua, that he had seen worse cases than ours, with feet blue up to the ankles, and that they had only been amputated up to the first joint!

He said that the doctors at Mendoza were very experienced in dealing with such cases and that they avoided amputations wherever possible. In fact everybody did their best to raise our morale and, with the help of the wine, we almost believed them. They now proposed to give us injections.

"What do you think?" asked Lucien, suspiciously.

I asked what they proposed to inject us with, and they replied, "Acetyl-choline". As this was a well known vasodilator, I raised no objection and agreed to an injection forthwith as an example. The attendant had prepared four syringes and tried to inject Robert, who obstinately refused.

"Guy, tell them I'm all right; they won't listen to me."

In order not to disappoint the sympathetic dentist (he was a dental surgeon), I persuaded Edmond to have two injections to make up for Robert's refusal. We now began to hear talk of departure, it was a five hours' journey on mule-back to Puente del Inca. While the soldiers got the mules ready, we put on our boots. Then we noticed that they were tying a man on to the back of a mule wrapped in a white blanket. We had no idea who he might be, but eventually found out that he was an Italian suffering from mountain sickness and that they were taking him down to Inca.

At half-past one we said good-bye to everybody and started off accompanied by sergeants Darvich and Labarta. We made our way down the almost dried-up river-bed of the Horcones Valley, which was about half a mile wide. The snow-water coming from the Horcones Glacier meandered through banks of gravel and the clear blue water splashed pleasantly over the stones.

Every now and again we came across the bleached bones of dead mules. Soon we approached Confluencia and the little streams increased in number, forming small lakes. The path closed in and wound down amid banks of moraine, at the bottom of the gorge flowed the Horcones torrent which we had to cross.

Clouds of dust on the other side announced the arrival of another caravan, in a few minutes we recognised Réné and Suzanne on their way down from Base Camp to Inca. They saw us at the same time and waited for us at the junction of the two paths. Darvich had already crossed the stream and it was now the turn of the Italian. The mule stumbled and the man fell heavily into the torrent. I said to Lucien:

"He's had it this time, if the fall hasn't killed him, he's bound to drown!"

"Oh, well, if he does, at least we won't be slowed up so much!"

We crossed the torrent, hardly looking at the lamentable form which Darvich and Labarta dragged out of the water. Our reaction to this incident was quite sincere, and the life or death of this unfortunate individual left us quite indifferent. I suddenly realised that we were still under the influence of the risks we had run and our sensibilities were still blunted. We caught up with Réné and Suzanne on the crest of the moraine. Réné came towards us, limping. His eyes were sunken, his face drawn and he had a week's growth of beard.

"Well," he said.

"Fine, it's in the bag."

"Yes, I know that, but the frostbite; is it serious?"

"Well, I don't want to sound too pessimistic, but as regards our feet, we're just like Herzog and Lachenal were, with the exception of Robert, who's in the clear."

"You're sure."

"I'm afraid so, all our toes are blue and Edmond and Lucien have got frozen hands as well. Don't let's waste any time but get on down to Inca. I hope the doctor's there, he'll be able to tell us all about it."

The path wound along the left bank of the Horcones river, and an hour later we crossed it again to reach the pastures surrounding Horcones Lake. About twenty bulls were grazing close to the path. "I don't like the look of them much," said Lucien.

"Don't worry, if you don't look at them they won't look at you."

"Oh you're all right, you're dressed in blue, but what about my red coat?"

"Oh, that doesn't matter. Bulls are colour blind."

"Well, it would be damn silly to have got this far only to be savaged by a bull."

We crossed the field safely without incident, and were met at end of the carriage road to Lake Horcones by an army command car close to which we could see Dr. Antinucci and Lieutenant Ramazzi. After an effusive greeting we got off the mules and entered the car. During the journey to Inca we plied the doctor with questions: "Is it serious? Are you going to amputate? How are Adrien and Pierre?"

The doctor replied as well as he could to this barrage and said quite shortly: "No amputations!"

We drew up in the courtyard of the military post and were soon served by soldiers with steaming bowls of café-au-lait. Without further ado we showed our feet to the doctor who examined them with a comforting smile. After the examination was over we mounted to the first floor where we found Adrien and Pierre lying in twin beds. As we entered they turned their bronzed faces towards us and exclaimed:

"Here you are at last, we've been waiting some time for you, we got here at noon!"

We went round the beds and shook hands. Adrien's face was swollen and cracked and Pierre's ears were mis-shapen, owing to the action of frost which had enlarged the lobes to three times their normal size.

"And what have you been doing?" said Edmond. "You look as if you'd had ten rounds with somebody?"

"Well, at least you look all right; you're standing up like a ramrod!"

"On the contrary," said Edmond, "with the sole exception of Robert, all our toes are like bits of charcoal."

A soldier entered with a tray of glasses and bottles of beer.

"Jolly good," remarked Lucien, "you're well organised I see."

"Bring some more bottles," said Edmond.

Glass in hand, we asked our friends to tell us about their descent.

"Will you tell them?" said Pierre.

"No, you tell them, please," said Adrien.

Pierre finished his beer and commenced:

"By the time I had coiled the rope I was last off the summit. It took some time as it was very tangled. I started down the 'canaleta' with Edmond and Adrien about fifty feet in front of me. I knew that my eyes must have been affected by the sun for I could not distinguish the colours of their anoraks very distinctly. Further on I slipped and fell and when I got up I found I was all entangled in the cord of my piton hammer which was still fastened round my neck. I didn't waste any time, but cut the cord and threw the hammer away. You may remember, chaps, that it was a hammer that I had had specially made for me." He uttered a sigh of regret.

"I understand perfectly," interrupted Robert. "Do you remember when we reached the arête that the fixed rope which we had recovered jammed behind us? I couldn't bother to get it loose and cut it with my axe. Well, now I wish I hadn't."

"Stop telling your life-story," broke in Lucien, "let him go on."

"Well, it was just then that I found out that there was something queer about my feet. Frankly that knocked me back a bit and I felt depressed. However, I told myself that it was no use worrying about it and the best thing to do was to get down to the hut as soon as possible and get them massaged.

"It was beginning to get dark, and I saw you traverse to the right, but when I reached the place where you had disappeared I could find no trace of a path so I went straight on down. It was small scree thereabouts so I did a sitting glissade to save time and energy. I could see the valley right below me and assumed that Plaza de Mulas could not be far away, so to save time I decided to continue on down and not to look for the refuge. I was sure that there would be a stream in the valley and the idea of being able to drink my fill and wash my face spurred me on.

"Every now and them I shouted and suddenly I saw lights below me and at the same time I heard faint cries from behind. On turning round I realised that I must have passed the hut. The lights below were still shining though intermittently, so I went on. I had visions of a farm with plenty of fresh milk and I remember saying 'it must be very late, I really can't wake them up'. But I was terribly thirsty."

The door opened and a soldier entered with more beer.

"You see, he understood my Spanish," said Edmond brightly.

"Lovely grub," said Lucien; "bring some more!"

Pierre continued:

"In the end I tried a standing glissade down some snow but had forgotten about my feet and finished up on my tummy. I must have looked funny in the dark! When I picked myself up in the rocks I found that I'd lost a glove. As I was looking for it I heard somebody call out close by, I replied and a few moments later Didi turned up. He gave me a glove and we went on down together. The lights got closer, Adrien was ahead of me and I heard voices. In spite of my feet I started to run in case Adrien had already started drinking. Somebody appeared out of the darkness, flung his arms round my neck and cried "*Viva Francia*". It was Darvich and I was so glad to see him that I felt like crying. It was only then that I realised that we were not at a hut, just five men bivouacing in sleeping bags on the ground. I believe they had a sick Italian with them."

"Ah, that explains everything," said I, "he came down with us, I don't quite know what was the matter with him but he did his best to get himself drowned in the river."

At this point we opened the bottles and slaked our thirst. Pierre went on:

o   197

"All we wanted to do was to get down to Plaza de Mulas as soon as possible. Eventually, after a long discussion, they saddled four mules and we went down, accompanied by Darvich and a very nice chap with white hair."

"He was at Plaza de Mulas this morning," said Robert; "he's a meteorologist from Mendoza, called Raskin."

"We got to Plaza de Mulas at half-past one in the morning. Everybody was most kind and massaged our feet, and we had plenty of drink. At dawn they put us on mules again and we came down here."

Just then Lieutenant Ramazzi came to ask us to dine at the Hotel de la Fondation and, much to our regret, we had to leave our friends for the time being.

It was a gay meal, with plenty to drink. The manager provided champagne and we drank toasts to Aconcagua, France and Argentina, after which we retired to bed slightly intoxicated.

Our feet were beginning to hurt now. We went to say good night to Dr. Antinucci, who said: "Wait a bit, I haven't finished with you yet." We understood better what he meant when he returned in a few moments accompanied by a soldier carrying a tray loaded, not with beer this time, but with syringes of various kinds. . . .

"What do you think of this?" said Adrien, as we got into bed.

It was extremely pleasant to be in bed between sheets and in a warm room. I stretched out voluptuously—no worries about the morrow. Half asleep, I replied:

"We certainly can't see the Southern Cross, like we used to every night, but at least it's more comfortable and much less cold than the ice and snow."

Chapter Six

DARK DAYS

(*Written in hospital*)

February 27th

M Y first thought when I awoke was for my feet. I had hoped that there would have been an improvement during the night, but they were as blue as ever. I hastily hid them at the bottom of the bed and turned my attention to the café-au-lait which had just been brought in.

Robert and Réné were kept busy running to and fro between our two rooms, and they told us that bad weather had at last arrived on Aconcagua. Here, however, it was fine and the sun shone into our room through the pretty cretonne curtains. Dr. Antinucci came in full of amiability and vitality, and asked if we had had a good night. He then subjected us to a veritable orgy of injections, which I must admit he did remarkably well—penicillin to ward off any possible infection and glucose serum to "pick us up". He renewed Pierre and Adrien's bandages and bandaged me up as well.

After lunch we had a siesta, and awoke much refreshed. We were so dried up after our climb that we just could not drink enough and constantly called for beer, but the soldiers refused to give us any more. We complained to the doctor, who said he was not surprised, as it was he who had stopped our supply.

"Do you realise that between you you've got through twenty-eight bottles since last night? Yesterday was different, but from today on no more alcohol. Tomorrow you will be at the hospital."

The Ministry of War had decided that we were to be treated at the military hospital at Mendoza. We were quite pleased to hear this, for we had been given to understand that they did not do any amputations there. During the afternoon we talked over the events of the last few days, but we needed time before we could visualise it —it was all too recent in our memories.

During the evening Cassis came in to see us to thank us for the new 200-foot nylon rope which Robert had given him. I asked him his views on the temperature likely to be experienced on the South Face, and he said that on the last three nights we were there it must have been in the neighbourhood of $-22°$ F. This was quite enough to explain our frostbite.

February 28th

We set out for the hospital at half-past nine in the morning. Lieutenant Ramazzi and Réné came down with us, leaving Robert and Suzanne behind. We got to Mendoza during the afternoon, and were carried into the hospital and set down before a door marked *"Cirugia"*.

"I may not know much Spanish, but I know enough to understand that," said Lucien; "it means 'Surgery'."

The door opened, and I was carried in to the room, where an imposing array of doctors and orderlies were waiting. All they did, however, was to undo my bandages and make a number of notes, after which I was placed on a trolley and wheeled out. My friends had a shock when they saw me.

"What did they do to you?" asked Edmond uneasily.

I turned my head and said quickly: "Nothing at all; it's all right."

They took me into a large room with two beds, and a few minutes later Edmond joined me. The room had a high ceiling and white-tiled walls.

"It's not very bright," I said to Edmond. "Fortunately we shan't be here for more than a month."

"Don't you believe it—I know these doctors; it'll be longer than that."

Adrien and Pierre were in a room opposite to ours and Lucien was next door. The chief medical officer came to see us and spoke a little French. We asked him what there was for dinner, and were somewhat depressed to learn that all we would get was soup, stewed fruit and mineral water.

What with this unappetising meal, the dreary room and the penicillin injection which followed, our morale descended to a very low level. Edmond aptly summed up the situation:

"There's no mistake about it, we're in hospital all right!"

Next day we were subjected to injections of all kinds, one after another. A number of doctors visited us, including Lieutenant-Colonel Ramon Notti, who was in charge of our welfare. The first week passed rapidly enough, and we began to learn a few rudimentary words of the Spanish language.

René went to Puente del Inca at the beginning of this week. As far as we were concerned the expedition was over, but Robert and he had the job of evacuating Base Camp and Camps I and II.

We now began to receive news from home, including official and private telegrams of congratulation. We began to make friends. Officers, N.C.O.s and men, as well as orderlies, all did their best to help us in any way possible. For the first time we really began to get to know the people of Argentina, whose tact, cordiality and sympathy left nothing to be desired. We had visits from Argentine civilians every morning. We never had the slightest idea who they were, but they came in small groups, full of amiability, stayed a few minutes and then departed. The French residents of Mendoza had got us two radio sets and before long we were quite *au fait* with the daily programmes, which seemed to consist solely of tangos, tangos and yet more tangos!

One day we had a surprise visit from the French Military Attaché, Colonel Bernard, who had made a special journey from Buenos Aires. He brought a large number of packets of French cigarettes "in the diplomatic bag", he said, and also a bottle of three-star brandy. Although alcohol was still prohibited, we could not refrain from drinking his health in it. A day or two later we were very astonished to receive a visit from two old friends from Fontainebleau, who were on a journey by car through South America.

Our toes were now quite black and mummified and looked like pieces of ebony. Doctor Notti tested them by tapping them gently with his forceps, whereupon they gave out a dry sound, something like that produced by castanets. He told us that we would lose scarcely anything at all—the very tips at the most. He was so convincing that we believed him. He said we had only to wait, and nature would do the rest, sloughing off the dead flesh in course of time.

This morning we were given new temperature charts, as we had completed our first month of hospital treatment. At the same time Suzanne, Réné and Robert returned, and they told us about the evacuation of the various camps.

"Evacuating Camp II was a hell of a job," said Robert. "We had a day of it, I can tell you."

"You're telling me," said Réné. "I've never suffered so much during the whole of my mountain career, which amounts to twelve years. I was neither in training nor acclimatised, and I really thought I should never get beyond the Towers. It was just about all I could manage to get to Camp II."

"In the end," said Robert, "we brought back everything, except the fixed ropes. We were carrying too much to rappel, so we had to leave them behind."

April

Dr. Notti gave us permission for our first outing, so one Saturday morning we went out with Lieutenants Allue and Ramazzi to see the festival of gathering the grapes. There was a parade of carts, and in the evening a beauty contest to elect the Queen of the Vines. Our feet were painful now, but we got so fed up with staying in our rooms that we took every opportunity of going out. The somewhat difficult question of transport was finally solved by Robert, who carried us in turn on his back. We even went to the pictures in this way! Naturally, everyone in Mendoza knew about us by this time, and we were continually stopped in the street and asked about the progress of our feet. Every Sunday our friend Lieutenant Allue used to take us to a football match. The first time we went a special stand had been prepared for us and our arrival was announced by loud speaker amid tumultuous applause. The French flag was hoisted alongside the Argentine national colours and the band played the "Marseillaise".

Our feet were now going through a new stage. There was a definite line of demarcation between the dead flesh and the rest of the foot. Some of us noticed that our toes were beginning to divide into sections of different lengths. All this was fairly painful, and we became extremely sensitive to changes in the weather; sometimes we sat up all night smoking to take our minds off our feet, and next day it usually rained!

In spite of all this we did not discontinue our outings. We had discovered a new sport—shooting, which we practised with great regularity.

Last week of April

We had now been exactly two months in hospital, and nobody could tell when we were likely to leave. We were beginning to get rather depressed, and were very glad when we received an invitation to the annual cocktail party of the Andean Club of Mendoza. It was a most enjoyable evening—few speeches and much drink! At half-past two in the morning I roused myself from my nebulous condition and remembered that we must not get back to hospital too late. When I mentioned this to the others, they became a little abusive and reminded me that the evening was only just beginning and that one was only young once, etc. Eventually I persuaded them to have one for the road and we set off for the hospital.

Our arrival did not pass unnoticed, for while Adrien hiccuped his way down the corridor, Lucien and Edmond, stretched side by side on the floor, were singing the chorus of Heaven know's what drinking-song at the top of their voices. We gained our respective rooms, and a few moments later noises were heard from the room which Edmond shared with a young Argentine recovering from an appendicitis operation.

"I think Edmond must be ill," said Lucien.

Meanwhile the frightened Argentine was trying to attract the attention of the orderlies by knocking violently on the wall with a stick.

"We really must shut him up," said Lucien decisively. "If he goes on like this he'll wake up the entire hospital" (as if he had not already done so!).

Lucien went off down the corridor on all fours, and we heard a fierce argument break out next door: "Shut up, you clot, or I'll crown you" (the blows from the stick ceased).

I heard loud roars of laughter from Edmond and Lucien and the latter reappeared in a hilarious state.

"I shut him up, you see."

"Maybe; but what about Edmond?"

"Edmond? Oh, he's in fine form. His stomach was a bit upset, but he's all right now."

Unfortunately the young Argentine had his revenge next day, for he reported us to Dr. Notti, who forthwith forbade any more outings, since we did not know how to behave ourselves! We let the storm blow itself out, principally because we were not in a position to do anything else.

Three days after this memorable evening we had another session of bandaging. Usually this operation took only a few minutes. Today, however, the doctors were more than half an hour in Pierre and Adrien's room, orderlies kept coming and going, somebody took in a powerful light and I could see through the glass door that they had still not started to put back the bandages.

The door opened and Robert came out, looking upset.

"What's going on?" I asked.

"They've just done it to Pierre and Adrien. I think you'd better be prepared; it's your turn next."

"What on earth do you mean? Tell me!"

"Notti has just cut off all Pierre's toes and three of Didi's."

We had no time to say any more, for the trolley arrived, preceded by the Chief Medical Officer, Dr. Notti himself, with two other doctors. They took off my bandage, and the doctor tried to twist off one of the toes of my right foot, which was partly loose. Unfortunately the bone was still sound. Notti shook his head and said, "Cut." I clenched my teeth so as not to cry out, Robert held me in his arms.

"Don't give way, Guy; Pierre never said a word, so you mustn't let us down!"

There was a sharp snipping sound and an agonising pain shot through my foot. I stifled a groan by biting on Robert's coat—I had lost my first toe.

"Ah well," said Lucien, "that's what they call 'to fall alone'. As I've only got three toes I can move, I claim the right to the next session."

We all took lunch in the room occupied by the two

who had lost the most toes. In spite of everything we had quite good appetites, except for Robert, who said his stomach was upset.

Next week Lucien lost three or four toe-joints.

Our third month in hospital began a few days ago. We were getting very tired of it all. We wanted to get away and return to France, and the dull autumnal weather did not help matters. Dr. Notti went off to Buenos Aires for a few days, and on his return they proposed to operate on Edmond, Lucien and myself under anæsthetic. He assured us that the end of our hospital treatment was near and that we could leave a fortnight after the operations.

May 13th

We were operated on this morning. In spite of the fatigue and pain inseparable from this surgical function, we were pleased, as we realised that we had taken an important step towards what we looked upon as our freedom. When the bandages were removed I was quite taken aback, as I had never expected that the removal of some toes could so change the appearance of a foot.

Lucien was very depressed at the loss of a number of finger-joints. We did our best to cheer him up by reciting stories of workmen who had had amputations and nevertheless had been able to follow their usual occupation.

Some time previously we had been invited by Lieutenant-Colonel Ugarte to spend a few days at Campo Los Andes. The Colonel had climbed Aconcagua more than once and it was he who had constructed the huts on the ordinary route. Dr. Notti allowed us to accept this invitation, with the exception of Pierre and Edmond, who had not sufficiently convalesced. We spent a wonderful week there in the officers' mess and were treated right royally. There was a terrific party the night before we left, at which we participated in a sort of Argentine barbecue. The week had passed all too quickly, and when we returned to hospital it was like coming back to a prison. Fortunately we were able to go out every day, and we spent most of our time with Réné and Suzanne at the hotel. Dr. Notti now committed himself regarding our departure and said that we could leave the first week of June—in ten days' time.

Life now began to get somewhat hectic, consisting of a succession of cocktail parties, receptions and dinners. Under the auspices of L'Alliance Française we gave our first public lecture, in the course of which we gave a detailed description of our ascent.

At last, on June 7th, we received our marching orders. Adrien and I had been to the pictures, and got back at half-past seven. We had hardly entered our room before we heard loud roars coming from Edmond next door.

"Something must have really happened this time," said Adrien; "let's go and see."

As we opened the door we were greeted by Pierre, who shouted excitedly:

"Here you are at last! The planes for Buenos Aires arrived this afternoon and the take-off is at half-past nine. You've just got time to get ready."

As it turned out only the first part of this information was true, for the departure was actually fixed for next morning. We immediately had a celebration and kept the orderly quite busy coming in to tell us to make less noise and stop singing, as we were disturbing the other patients.

We were up at six o'clock next morning, for somehow or other we had been unable to do any packing the previous night. Just before the transport arrived to take us to the airport we made a round of rather tearful farewells among the hospital staff who had been so kind to us during our enforced stay with them.

At last we were off, the door opened, the guard presented arms and we left the hospital for the last time. We drove along the magnificent avenue of Boulogne-sur-

Mer, named after General San Martin, who is buried at
Boulogne in France. The vines of Mendoza were already
turning and autumn tints were everywhere. The first
dead leaves were falling, announcing the coming winter,
which we were leaving behind in exchange for spring in
France.

GLOSSARY

À cheval.	Astride a ridge as on horseback.
Arête.	Ridge, generally one of the main ridges of a mountain.
Bergschrund.	A large crevasse separating the upper slopes of a glacier from the ice or rock above.
Col.	Pass.
Cornice.	Overhanging mass of snow or ice along a ridge.
Couloir.	Rock, ice or snow gully.
Crampons.	Metal frame with spikes fitted to the boots for use on hard snow or ice.
Crevasse.	Fissure or crack in a glacier.
Étrier.	Literally stirrup. A short rope ladder used in artificial climbing.
Foehn.	A warm wind from the south.
Gendârme.	Rock tower on a ridge.
Karabiner.	Metal spring-loaded clip which can be fixed to a rope or piton.
Marteau-piolet.	"Hammer-axe." A short combined piton hammer and ice axe.
Moraine.	Stones and debris brought down by a glacier.
Névé.	Compacted snow at the head of a glacier.
Nieves penitentes.	Ice pinnacles formed by ablation. Often reaching to the height of a man, they are said to resemble penitents.
Pitons.	Metal spikes for driving into rock or ice. (Broches are short pitons with extra thin blades. Extraplats are pitons with U-shaped blades.)
Rappel.	Also known as roping down. Method of descending steep pitches by means of a doubled rope.
Séracs.	Ice towers, mainly found in ice falls.
Verglas.	Thin coating of ice on rock.